How I Have

How I Have Changed

Reflections on Thirty Years of Theology

Edited by Jürgen Moltmann

TRINITY PRESS INTERNATIONAL

Harrisburg, Pennsylvania

Translated by John Bowden from the German
Wie ich mich geändert habe,
ed. Jürgen Moltmann, Published 1997 by
Christian Kaiser/Gütersloher Verlagshaus, Gütersloh

© Christian Kaiser/Gütersloher Verlagshaus, Gütersloh
1997

Translation © John Bowden 1997

Trinity Press International
PO Box 1321
Harrisburg, PA 17105

Trinity Press International is a division of The Morehouse Group.

First Published 1997 by
SCM Press Ltd.
9-17 St. Albans Place
London N1 0NX

Typset by Regent Typsetting, London

Library of Congress Cataloging-in-Publication Data

Wie ich mich geändert habe. English
How I have changed : reflections on thirty years of theology /
edited by Jürgen Moltmann
    p. cm.
    ISBN 1-56338-241-5
    1. Theology, Doctrinal—History—20th century—Congresses.
2. Theologians—Germany—Congresses. I. Moltmann, Jürgen.
II. Title.
BT28.W4813   1998
230'.09'045-dc21   97-39107
                                                                     CIP

Printed in the United States of America

98 99 00 01 02 03   10 9 8 7 6 5 4 3 2 1

Contents

Welcome

Jürgen Moltmann

The idea for this symposium of our theological generation comes from my wife. We have been thinking about it for years, and are delighted that today it has become reality. We are more than grateful that, without exception, all those whom we invited accepted our invitation. We grievously miss our friend Fred Herzog of Duke University, Durham, North Carolina, who died quite unexpectedly in September 1995. We are particularly pleased, though, that his wife Kristin Herzog has come. Unfortunately, Wolfhart Pannenberg, who is a quite essential part of our theological generation, had to withdraw at short notice. The day before yesterday, Hans-Eckehard Bahr had a circulatory collapse and sends greetings to the gathering from his sickbed.

Why this symposium? We wanted to look back over the last more or less thirty years and ask what has become of our new approaches after Barth and Rahner, Bultmann and Tillich. With what expectations did we begin? Why have we reacted so differently to the challenges of the time? What has changed our theological perspectives over these years, or left them unchanged? And what unresolved problems are we leaving behind for the next theological generation? What fundamental questions concern us today, and what questions do we have for one another? Here is an opportunity to raise them and suggest answers. We have deliberately also invited theologians who do not work in theological faculties, because we are convinced that theology is not just done in universities.

'How I Have Changed'. Of course this title echoes the

series of articles 'How My Mind Has Changed' which have appeared decade by decade in the Chicago *Christian Century* and to which some of us have contributed. But it is also prompted by Bert Brecht's well-known story about Herr Keuner. After many years Herr Keuner met an old acquaintance in the street, 'But you haven't changed at all,' was the acquaintance's greeting. And Herr Keuner went pale. We shall see which of us 'goes pale'!

We are grateful to Hans Norbert Janowski for being the presenter and chairman of this symposium. In particular we must keep to the timings he has set, so that he does not seem like the tamer in a cage of wild animals. We have planned three rounds of discussion, each of ninety minutes. The speakers each have twenty minutes for a short theological biography and theological message. After that, each time we have half an hour for cross-questioning and questions from the audience. The last round will take place before the television cameras. I am grateful that so many people have come, and hope that you and we will find that our expectations have been exceeded. The time is favourable and the opportunity is unique!

First Round

Eberhard Jüngel
Jürgen Moltmann
Dorothee Sölle

Eberhard Jüngel

Ladies and gentlemen, you see that I am rather pale – and that is not just because it was a short night. I am rather pale because in fact I have changed relatively little, indeed hardly at all. I am of the perverse view that my teachers still have rather more to say than I have and that the potential of their theology is not yet exhausted. Therefore although not to have changed seems to be a fault, and immutability does not seem to be a compliment even for God, I cannot give a very good account of changes that have affected me. However, there is a series of unforgettable situations, encounters, experiences which have recognizably influenced me and shaped me. Without them, unless I am completely mistaken, I would not be what I am today. And I would now like to talk about these, if you are prepared to listen, despite the misleading title under which I am speaking.

Here I shall be limiting myself to my life as a theologian. Certainly it is largely identical with my daily life. But in the life of a theologian, too, there is more than what is of public interest. For example, that in the course of time I have become a passable cook has a definitely political cause, but that cause need not be of interest to my guests as long as they do not suffer from the consequences of my cooking. I regard the view which is increasingly spreading throughout Europe, that everything in a person's life is of general interest and therefore has to be open to public investigation, as a dangerous failure to recognize the personal dignity of human beings. This view presumably derives from a Calvinism which spied on the private life of Christians. A person's dignity is more than what is worth publishing. The individual is ineffable, thank God!

The event, or rather the chain of events, which has recently moved me more than anything else is eminently political, the collapse of the Socialist system in Eastern Europe. This chain of events, which is also making a deep mark on the history of Germany, has made me aware how much my former experiences in East Germany have left a permanent stamp on me. So in an attempt to review my theological identity, for better or worse I must return to my beginnings.

No questions about 'religion' were asked in the home in which I grew up, and my desire to study theology came up against the anxious astonishment of my mother and the resolute opposition of my father. The fact that nevertheless I held to my purpose and finally achieved it can certainly also be explained in terms of the doubtless adolescent opposition of a son to his father's authority. But that is not all. There was a far deeper experience which was crucial to my decision and which has continued to influence me to the present day. That was the discovery of the Protestant Church as the only place within Stalinist society accessible to me at that time in which one could hear and speak the truth with impunity. Perhaps that was also true of the cabaret, at least of a particularly bold and particularly crafty cabaret. In Socialist society the cabaret and the church played something like the role of the jester. And the jester is the only one who can speak the truth in a mendacious society in a jesting way.

What a liberating experience this was by comparison with the ideological and political tyranny which prevailed at school! Friends were arrested; I myself was interrogated several times by the security services and taken to court – simply because we dared to say what we thought. One day before my school-leaving examination, directly before the workers' revolt in 1953, I was removed from my school as an

4

'enemy of the republic'. My fellow pupils were required immediately to break off all contact with us. As I left the hall of the Humboldt School in Magdeburg, in which however a very different spirit from that of Humboldt now prevailed, the honest men and women among the teachers there turned away in helpless silence. This was a symbolic scene in which the truth of the sentence from Cicero which these same teachers had instilled in us dawned on me like a flash. *Cum tacent, clamant*: by keeping silent, they cry out. However, in the Christian church one was free to break through that oppressive silence and the pressure to lie, which was becoming increasingly marked. Here people dared to witness to the truth of the gospel, and to do so in the political situation in such a way that the liberating power of this truth could also be experienced in a very secular, indeed a very political, way. 'You wil know the truth, and the truth will make you free' (John 8.32). Since that time, this New Testament statement has become one of my favourites.

So when today we see the old system totally collapse like a house of cards, and begin to analyse everything, asking why this Socialism ultimately failed, we have to take seriously as a decisive cause its objective mendacity. Far from expressing an opposition to Socialism in principle, I cannot close my eyes to the mendacious way in which Socialist ideals were put into action in power politics. One can discuss Socialist ideals, but these also include the possibility of resistance. And resistance was not allowed. The monopoly of truth claimed by the Party and imposed with the force of the state was directed against the truth itself, and produced a perversion of thought to which those involved necessarily fell victim. The compulsion to deceive not only the public but also oneself dominated all spheres of social life – down to economic decisions. And so it inevitably seemed like a revolution when Gorbachev began to call for 'Glasnost', clarity, insight, truth.

Now what has all this to do with my theological thought?

5

Only that on the basis of those experiences of the church in which I encountered it as an institution of liberating truth – from a paternal veto here, a paternal veto there – I became a theologian, and to this day I have never seriously regretted it. When my dear colleagues Johann Baptist Metz and Jürgen Moltmann and my – if you will excuse the expression – friend-foe or foe-friend Dorothee Sölle later began the enterprise of a 'political theology' and made it highly influential, on the basis of those experiences I insisted that the political relevance of Christian faith consists first and last in its capacity for truth and its obligation to truth. The political action imposed on the church is aimed above all at giving the truth its due.

So I pursued further postulates in the European context initially with some reservations, because I sensed a new political servitude, as it were a left-wing clericalization of society, in a programme which wanted to obligate every Christian theologically to one and only one quite definite political option, or even elevate the Socialist revoution to a theological principle. On the other hand, I found the supporters of 'political theology' far too abstract in concrete issues of real life: they seemed to me rather to simulate concreteness in the form of all kinds of activism. That, at any rate, is how things initially seemed to me in the European context. But the significance that the 'theology of liberation' gained for me in the context of the scandalous social injustice in the so-called Third World and in the context of South African racism taught me better. The immeasurable shame that I felt as a white man in South African townships convinced me utterly that it can also be permissible for Christians, indeed even be obligatory for Christians, to oppose unjust systems not only with ideas and words but also with works, and therefore if need be with violence. However, here the believer must decide, on his or her own individual responsibility. One may not be compelled theologically by

6

others to be violent; in such a case one make one's very own, free, decision.

However, in this connection I was annoyed that something like a theology of liberation had evidently not been considered for those people who were oppressed in the world of the 'Socialist experiment'. It was an ecumenical scandal that even in Geneva, the seat of the World Council of Churches, where people named injustice in other parts of the world so boldly for what it was, and even gave practical support to resistance movements, they were by contrast blind to the end about conditions e.g. in Rumania. Diplomacy towards the Orthodox Churches may explain it, but it is unforgivable. And we can only hope that this dark shadow will not obscure the indisputably great achievements of the ecumenical movement.

While I was not very impressed with the political realizations of Marxism, the atheism to which Marxist theory committed its adherents represented a challenge which still occupies me today. It is already worth reflecting on the way in which people in the German Democratic Republic were evidently more influenced by the atheistic option of Marxism than by its political power and economic form. Did political pressure here simply bring out something for which the ground had long been prepared? At any rate, the large number of Germans living beyond the Elbe who belong to no religious community speaks for itself. But regardless of all statistics, the encounter with atheism persistently stimulated my thought from the beginning of my teaching activity.

A propos teaching. I became a theological teacher literally overnight as a result of the building of the Berlin Wall. When Erich Honecker built the Berlin Wall on the orders of Walter Ulbricht and thus firmly cemented the division of Germany, the students of the Kirchliche Hochschule living in East Berlin were cut off from their professors, who lived in West Berlin. In order to meet the emergency which thus arose, Kurt

Scharf, who later became a bishop, appointed me a theological teacher. I had only gained my doctorate in theology a few weeks before and therefore was hopelessly badly prepared. It was the same for my friend Hermisson, and the then Bishop of Magdeburg, my friend Demke, found the same thing. A time of hard lucubrations began. What nights we worked! Often I did not know in the evening what I would be lecturing on next morning. Nowadays, the theology which came into being in this way would be called 'contextual'. And it was, in so far as I asked myself how talk of God can prove its truth in a situation stamped by atheism. It seemed me too cheap simply to demonize atheism or to expose it as a pseudo-religion. Rather, I felt obliged to understand atheism better than it understood itself, and attempted theologically to get to the bottom of it. Here I know that I am still one with Dorothee Sölle in believing that the dark word of the death of God is a genuinely theological word.

It soon became clear to me that what was manifesting itself in an extremely intolerant form in the Eastern block was simply what was shaping the modern and postmodern world in a much more sublime way. On closer examination I recognized that religion and atheism need not be mutually exclusive. Thus the basic atheistic trait of the age seems to be something different from the religionslessness diagnosed by Bonhoeffer. Had not Schleiermacher already observed 'that a religion without God can be better than another with God'? The new forms of religion which have sprung up in recent years – in Europe we largely have a vagabond form of religion – should not therefore be celebrated in over-hasty apologetics as the overcoming of atheism. At any rate, my concern is to discover an element of truth in atheism which is at least as strong as metaphysics with a theistic constitution. That explains why I could only resolutely oppose the old and most recent apologetic, which denounces atheism as a deficient mode of being human.

Quite apart from the fact that my brother, who is a genuine atheist and not only older, but also stronger, than I am, would probably still threaten to give me a good hiding if I were to call him a defective human being. What gives us the right to assume that atheists are less human than pious Jews or Christians or Muslims or Buddhists? The proclamation of the justification of the godless can hardly thrive in the soil of such apologetic religious propaganda. Anyone who has to talk about the overcoming of godlessness by God will do better to take the atheist seriously as a particularly mature form of the *homo humanus*. And that human godlessness has been overcome by God exposing himself to death for us in the person of Jesus Christ – the death which is the wages of sin (Rom.6.23) – is the centre of the theology which I know myself to have been called to advocate.

Now a few remarks on the teachers who shaped me. There was a philosopher who instructed me in logic and logistics, Gerhard Stammler. There was my New Testament teacher and doctoral supervisor, Ernst Fuchs, who brought me and Rudolf Bultmann together and stimulated me to study Heidegger. In a semester spent 'illegally' outside East Germany, commuting between Zurich, Basel and Freiburg, I then heard Heidegger himself lecturing in Freiburg. At that time he was 'on the way to language'. Towards the end of his life I visited him once again and at the end of a long conversation asked him quite openly whether the condition of thought was not that of being 'on the way to God'. Heidegger replied, 'God – that is what is most worth thinking about. But here language fails . . .' Now I certainly didn't have this impression myself. At that time Gerhard Ebeling had introduced me to the thought of Luther, while in Basel Karl Barth made me familiar with his own thought. And Luther's concern for a new mode of theological language, and also Barth's theology, which flowed broadly from there and suffered more from a excess of argumentation, did not exactly give the

9

impression of a language which was failing. At first Barth regarded me as a kind of spy from the Bultmann school and for weeks viewed me with undisguised scepticism. But when in an unforgettable session of his small seminar I not only dared passionately to refute his criticism of Bultmann with the audacity of youth but at the same time interpreted a section from Barth's anthropology to his satisfaction, I was invited to another dispute in the late evening over a bottle of wine. And a few days later the whole of the *Church Dogmatics* appeared on the doorstep of my student lodging – with the dedication 'For Eberhard Jüngel on the way in God's beloved East Zone'.

There, in the German Democratic Republic, some years later, when I now had to give lectures on dogmatics myself and was looking round for helpful stimulation, I once again steeped myself in this *magnum opus* of my great teacher. And lo and behold, here within a theological discussion which was becoming increasingly short of breath, I discovered the long breath of a thought which expected something. Barth's theology was autochthonous. From it one could learn that a concentration on the truth attested in the Bible is the best presupposition for giving the present world its spiritual and worldly due and keeping faith with the earth for the sake of heaven. A new involvement in the tradition opened up for me, which was one neither of disrespectful criticism nor of uncritical respect. And as a result of this I also developed an ecumenical breadth without which I simply cannot imagine any future theology. Above all, however, I was stimulated to think of God in terms of the event of his revelation, i.e. the event of his coming into the world, and thus of a God who leads us ever more deeply into the world – a God to whom nothing human is alien and who has come closer to humankind in the person of Jesus than humankind can get to itself.

This Augustinian *interior intimo meo* acquired a kind of

key function for my theological thought; it also opened the door towards mysticism, towards a strict mysticism. However, I concede that unlike others sitting here I have always really only looked through this door, and have not really gone through it. But that may happen. Perhaps I might also change in this respect, too.

A kind of closing remark. What has theology to offer? The answer, expressed as a slogan, is at the same time the scarlet thread which runs through my theological existence. Theology has enlightenment to offer. Not, however, enlightenment in the light of reason, nor as the enemy of the light of reason either. It has to offer enlightenment in the light of the gospel, and to do so in such a way that there is a critical dialogue with reason. And just as theology has to provide enlightenment in the light of the gospel, so, to use an old phrase, it has to rescue the endangered phenomena, 'saving the appearances'. In this sense creation has to be given its due.

In my judgment, this also involves not simply giving up the task of subduing the earth (Gen. 1.28), but perceiving it in such a way that there really is a *Dominium terrae*, whereas we have perceived that task in such a way as to make the *Dominium* an *Imperium*. Human beings must continue to rule if the world is not to be destroyed. At all events, it will be destroyed just as quickly if we cease to rule, as if we rule violently in reckless self-centredness. What we need is a form of control which is capable of controlling itself. If that can be achieved, then perhaps parables of the kingdom of heaven will also appear in our still unredeemed world. For this to happen, in my view it would be necessary for theology along with philosophy to develop something like a table of categories of evil. In our Tübingen theological discussions Ernst Bloch once complained vigorously that we did not have a table of categories of evil. Theology must attempt in the light of the gospel to outline something like a table of categories of evil, not to make us fascinated by evil, but to put it in its place with the sharp, sidelong glance which is what it deserves. One can fight evil only if one conceptualizes it with the strictest thought, in order then to put it in its place by bold action. True, that in itself does not bring about the beginning of the kingdom of heaven on earth. But it would prevent the earth from becoming hell. And God's will is to change us in this direction, so that earth does not become a hell. That is the will of the God who has overcome hell, death and the devil for ever and promised a life in freedom and peace. And what is a life in freedom and peace, if not the achieving of life together with God? To reflect thoughtfully and responsibly on faith in this God and hope for such a life together – in my view that is the task of a proper theologian. I have tried, and will always continue to try, to be a proper theologian. And I shall do so with pleasure.

Jürgen Moltmann

I come from a secular family of teachers in Hamburg. Far from being interested in religion and theology, I wanted to study physics and mathematics: Max Planck and Albert Einstein were the heroes of my youth. In the last week of July 1943, Hamburg was destroyed in a firestorm as a result of the British Royal Air Force's 'Operation Gomorrah'. 40,000 people perished. With my school class I was in a flak battery in the inner city as an auxiliary. It was wiped out, but the bombs which tore away the schoolfriend standing next to me spared me. In the night, for the first time I cried out to God. 'My God, where are you?', was my question. 'Why am I alive and not dead like the others?' During three years as a prisoner of war I looked for an answer, first in the Old Testament psalms of lamentation and then in the Gospel of Mark. When I came to Jesus' dying cry, I knew, 'There is your divine brother and redeemer, who understands you in your god-forsakenness.' I sought knowledge to give support to my existence and abandoned my interest in physics and mathematics to find it. Auschwitz and Hiroshima disturbed me deeply.

In England there was a Protestant theologians' camp, Norton Camp near Nottingham. There captive lecturers taught captive students. I began my theological study in 1947. We read and discussed from morning to night; we were looked after by the YMCA and supervised by the British army. The experiences of the life of a prisoner have left a lasting mark on me: the suffering and the hope which reinforce each other. When one grasps the courage to hope, the chains begin to hurt, but the pain is better than the resignation in which everything is a matter of indifference.

In 1948 I studied in Göttingen. Hans Joachim Iwand convinced me of the liberating truth of the Reformation doctrine of justification and the theology of the cross through a gripping series of lectures on Luther's theology (by candle-light, because of power cuts). Iwand aroused our theological passion, but for scholarly work we went to Ernst Wolf and Otto Weber. I got to know my wife there. Otto Weber supervised both our doctorates and became our friend. In 1952 I, too, had finished my thesis, and we married, but to begin with I had no connection with a church. The Protestant state churches, which had kept silent or rejoiced in the Hitler period, did not appeal to me. I was impressed only by the Confessing Church, with the Barmen Theological Declaration of 1934 and its clear Yes and No. However, it could not establish itself in the post-war period. When after 1945 Adenauer and Bishop Dibelius restored the old 1933 conditions, though these had not hindered Hitler and the German Christians, I joined the groups which succeeded the Confessing Church, the 'Brotherhoods' and the 'Society for Protestant Theology'. These were critical of both politics and the churches. At that time we were very Barthian and wanted to get away from the misalliances of 'throne and altar', 'faith and the bourgeoisie', 'religion and capitalism', characteristic of culture Protestantism, and move in the direction of 'Christ alone' and radical discipleship in the service of peace. 'Fight Nuclear Death', 'No Rearmament', 'No Contracts for Army Chaplains' were our slogans at the time.

The 'loss of the centre' seemed to be a precise description of the situation of Christianity, which had lost its bearings. So we sought 'the centre of scripture' and became exclusively christocentric, *solus Christus*. However, we got into difficulties with this narrow understanding of Barth and this 'Barmen orthodoxy' when we wanted to give positive answers to the political possibilities and cultural challenges of the post-war period.

Every 'centre' has a surrounding area, otherwise it is not a centre. In 1951, Dietrich Bonhoeffer's *Letters and Papers from Prison* led us out of the dilemma. In the way in which he opened up horizons we discovered 'true worldliness' and 'religionless Christianity'. After Karl Barth's monumental *Dogmatics*, I thought, there could be no more theology (just as there could be no more philosophy after Hegel), because he had said it all and said it so well. Then in 1957 I got to know the Dutch theologian Arnold van Ruler. He cured me of this misapprehension. I discovered the Reformed kingdom of God theology and the Dutch apostolate theology. As a community pastor in Wasserhorst, a suburb of Bremen, I read a good deal of Christoph Blumhardt, another approach to the kingdom of God theology.

In 1959, just after I had arrived at the Kirchliche Hochschule in Wuppertal, I published my first programmatic theological work, *The Community in the Horizon of the Lordship of Christ*. It was only thirty-five pages long and remained quite unknown. Reading it again today, I can discover most of my later ideas in this beginning: the messianic dimension, faithfulness to the earth, the inviting horizon of God's future, the theology of politics and secular preaching . . . Must I 'go pale'?

In 1960 I discovered Ernst Bloch's *The Principle of Hope*. I read it in the East German edition during a holiday in Switzerland and was so fascinated that I ceased to see the beauty of the mountains. My spontaneous impression was, 'Why has Christian theology let go of its most distinctive theme, hope?' After all, Bloch referred to the 'exodus and the messianic parts of the Bible'. And what has become of the earliest Christian spirit of hope for the kingdom of God in today's established Christianity? With my 1964 *Theology of Hope* I did not seek to be Bloch's 'heir'. Nor did I want to 'baptize' his *Principle of Hope*, as Barth in Basel suspected. Rather, I wanted to undertake a parallel action in

Christianity on the basis of its own presuppositions. Whereas Bloch regarded the modern Feuerbach-Marx atheism as a ground for hope, I began from the biblical history of God, exodus and resurrection. To his social utopias for the 'weary and heavy laden' and his utopias of justice for the 'humiliated and the injured' I added the eschatological horizon of the resurrection of the dead and saw the 'home-land of identity' first in the annihilation of death in the eternal presence of God. When we moved to Tübingen in 1967, we and Bloch became neighbours not only physically, but also in the spirit. I was not so much interested in his neo-Marxism, which attracted the left-wing students in 1968, as in his Jewish messianism, about which he had a low opinion at that time.

In 1964 I wrote *Theology of Hope* with pleasure and passion. For me it was a door to freedom, into God's 'open spaces'. But I did not know whether it was a theology about hope or in hope. The genitive allowed both. Later I found that hope should be the subject of theology. The book did not fit into any theological camp yet fitted into many. It was welcomed by secularists and pietists, black theologians and white liberals, Freemasons and Adventists. A perceptive review (by Horst Dohle) was found in the archives of the East German secret police. This said that the book was not for East German Christians; it was too revolutionary. An 'undigested Moltmann' was already being propagated at pastors' conferences, and he was 'worse than anyone'. In 1968 *Der Spiegel* included me among the 'children of protest': 'iron in pale Christian blood', 'obstreperous theo-logy of hope'.

The 1960s were years of a new awakening after the restorations of the post-war period: the Second Vatican Council in Rome, the Civil Rights Movement in the USA, Socialism with a human face in Czechoslovakia, the ecumenical enthusiasm of 'Behold I Make All Things New' in

Uppsala, and in West German politics Willy Brandt's 'Dare More Democracy'.

In 1967 Baptist Metz produced his *Theology of the World* and Hans Küng his liberating book *The Church*; in 1965 Eberhard Jüngel his *God's Being is in Becoming* and Dorothee Sölle her *Christ the Representative*. And before any of us, in 1961, Wolfhart Pannenberg wrote a theology of history from which the idea of 'anticipation' developed. Through Bloch I became involved in the Christian-Marxist dialogue of the Paulusgesellschaft. The last meeting took place in Marienbad in May 1967 and led us beyond the positions in which we had been bogged down, because we faced problems for which our various traditions had no answers.

1968 brought the climax and turning-point in the mood of a new awakening. Military intervention put an end to the Prague Spring. German and Polish troops also marched shamefully into Czechoslovakia. In Rome the encyclical *Humanae vitae* set a limit to the *aggiornamento* of the church; Catholic colleagues lost their posts. On 6 April Martin Luther King was shot. The black ghettoes burned. We were in America at that time. Rudi Dutschke was shot at a demonstration in Berlin. The student protest became more bitter. For me the political dream of a united Social Democratic Europe collapsed. The end in Prague paralysed me for weeks. At that time I was attempting to write an *Ethics of Hope* as a sequel to the *Theology of Hope*. It failed because I did not know whether reforms or revolution would improve circumstances. In the 'political theology' movement I attempted to work with a twofold strategy of the 'great alternative' and the many 'little alternatives', on the model of a Christianity of order there and a Christianity of the world here. But I did not have a detailed knowledge of the different fields of action and spheres of life. So nothing came of the *Ethics*.

Instead, I took up the threads of the theology of the cross again. After the grounding of Christian eschatology in the resurrection of the crucified Christ, the other side also had to be emphasized: the cross of the Risen Christ. In a culture which glorifies health, success and happiness and is blind to the suffering of others, recollection of the presence of the God in the crucified Christ can also open people's eyes. If God has raised that crucified Christ, then churches which take his name must dissolve their alliances with the powerful and seek solidarity with the humiliated who exist in the shadow of the cross. When I wrote *The Crucified God* – and I wrote it so to speak with my lifeblood – once again I saw the whole of theology in a focal point. For me the cross of Christ became the 'foundation and critique of Christian theology'. We had discussed sufficiently the question of the saving significance of the crucified Christ for us. So I reversed the question. What does the cross of Christ mean for God? Does an impassible God keep silent in heaven untouched by the suffering and death of his child on Golgotha, or does God himself suffer these pains and this death? The old metaphysical axiom of impassibility in the doctrine of God said that the Godhead is incapable of suffering. By contrast, I began from the essential passion of God – and I was by no means the first to do so. If God's existence is love, then God is also capable of suffering and shares in the suffering of his creatures. Thus Golgotha becomes the revelation of the suffering of the passionate God for us. This led me to discover that I shared views with other thinkers in a way which I had not expected. Abraham Heschel had interpreted the teaching of the Jewish prophets with the idea of the 'pathos of God'. Franz Rosenzweig found in the divine Shekinah God as the companion of his people, who shares in their suffering. In 1966 the Japanese theologian Kitamori conjured up the 'pain of God' and in 1944 Dietrich Bonhoeffer wrote in his Gestapo police cell, 'Only the suffering God can help.' In England there was a vigorous discussion of the passibility or impassibility of God in the nineteenth and twentieth centuries. Theology in Germany had not noted it taken part in it.

The Crucified God appeared in 1972 and was also my attempt to find an answer for a life in Germany 'after Auschwitz'. I came into close contact with the rising 'theology of liberation' in Latin America, and especially with Jon Sobrino, but also met with approval in Orthodox theology in Rumania. My link with the struggling and suffering church in Korea came into being, with the beginning of Minjung theology and also the mysticism of the cross of the Catholic Passionists. My interest was aroused in the experience of 'the dark night of the soul'. The prison cells of the martyrs and the monastic cells of the mystics are not very different. Academic critics again complained about my 'one-sidednesses' and pointed out how controversial and confrontational I was. In liberal and feminist theology the legend of my 'sado-masochistic God' who 'kills' his own son came into being. Before my eyes is another image. On 16 November 1989 six Jesuits and two women were brutally murdered in the University of San Salvador. The soldiers took the body of brother Ramon Moreno into the room of the absent Jon Sobrino. In his blood was found a book which had fallen down, *El Dios Crucificado*. Now it lies there under glass as a symbolic interpretation of the martyrdom of the brothers and sisters.

Now I must jump to another turning point in my life. It was at a conference in October 1977 in Mexico City with liberation theologians, black theologians and feminist theologians that I suddenly discovered: 'I don't belong anywhere, since I'm not oppressed, not black and not a woman. I can support these liberation movements and learn from them, but my existence is not in them. Granted, as far as I could, I've been involved in the peace movement and the ecological movement. The mass of students in Tübingen and ecumenical travels do not leave one much time. Feminist theology has influenced me more strongly than I realized, especially its psycho-social approach. So what should I do?' At that time I reflected on my regular business of systematic theology and between 1980 and 1995 wrote a series of 'systematic contributions to theology'. I wanted to overcome my 'one-sidednesses' and concentrate on long-term problems of theology. I no longer wanted to be so controversial. So I wrote 1. a social doctrine of the Trinity about the 'God who is rich in relationships'; 2. a sabbatical doctrine of creation in the face of the ecological crises which threaten; 3. a christology of the way and on the way; 4. a book about the spirit of life as '*élan vital*'; and 5. a Christian eschatology about the new beginning in the end.

These five books will be followed by one more on method. An American remarked that reflections on method are like clearing one's throat before a lecture. That can only go on as long as one can hold one's audience. I have always been interested only in the theological content. So I shall only 'clear my throat' briefly, as a postscript:

1. It should be possible to verify theological statements by one's own experiences or by empathy with the experiences of others, whether individual or collective. Experiences include praxis.

2. A person with different theological views should also be able to say to God what he or she says about God. It should also be possible to use theology for praying, lamenting or praising.

3. For me, from the start theology has been an adventure with an uncertain outcome, a voyage of discovery into an inviting mystery. My theological virtue has not been humility, but only curiosity and imagination for the kingdom of God.

4. In Europe we have a rich confessional background. But together 'with all Christianity on earth' – as Luther remarked

– we have a much richer ecumenical future. Concern with our own tradition must not hinder incorporation into the world-wide ecumenical community.

Dorothee Sölle

As I reflect on my generation and those who belong to it, I think first of the central event of German history in this century. This is perhaps even also the most central event to have played an essential part in my intrinsic development, this legacy of gas, violence, war and murder. I have never understood how a theology after Auschwitz can be precisely the same as before. That was one of the first points of my dismay at an untouched theology which kept saying the same thing in a different way, with no real relation to reality.

I come from an educated middle-class background, remote from the church. At home we were not particularly interested in whether a person went to church, but rather in whether a person was Nazi and antisemitic. That was important. That was how we distinguished people. Here there were dividing lines which were quite clear, and perhaps I have inherited something of this. Later it brought me all kinds of hostility in the church. As with Jürgen Moltmann, for me the decision to study theology came as a surprise; my liberal father was amazed and my mother laughed in a somewhat confused way, when after some semesters studying classics I decided to study theology. This decision was prompted by a theology teacher who was very important for me, Marie Veit. She was a pupil of Bultmann and came to our school as a very young woman. She gave fantastic lessons in which we read Heidegger and Sartre and discussed the New Testament no less frankly. When with all my impudence I attacked, say, the 'servile murmuring of Christians about the world to come', she had an inimitably shrewd manner of asking in a friendly way, 'Do you really mean Paul, or is it Luther, or where do you get that from?' So without putting me down, she taught me more than any teacher that I had later. She gave me the assurance, which she got from Bultmann, that one need not give up one's understanding at the church door but can quietly take it inside; that perhaps there was something more than what we perceived empirically. The other teachers I would like to mention are older writers, above all Kierkegaard and Pascal, who had thought out before me a Christianity by which I felt attracted, which I wanted to go into. But all this had little basis in the church as a real institution; I still found it a very problematical, difficult, even boring enterprise.

If you ask me how my mind has changed, I would say that nowadays I think about the church very differently. My attitude to the church has changed, or the church's attitude to me has changed, I'm not sure which. However, my hope for the resistance groups which have grown up within the churches as a result of the conciliar process has now become much greater. In all honesty I have to say that I often think that God's Spirit is not blowing in the faculties, but has long emigrated from them. But it is blowing among the women and men who block the transporting of nuclear waste or do other things that are necessary in our world. That is another form of dialogue into which I grew.

I began my theological studies in Göttingen. By that time Bultmann had retired, and I was very sad about that – I would very much have liked to go to Marburg and study with him. I went to Göttingen because of Friedrich Gogarten, who had written a book about the proclamation of Jesus Christ. This opened up to me a great deal of what Jesus, Paul and Luther said. There is a section in it on modern times which didn't seem to me to be adequate. But Gogarten was a teacher from whom I learned to think, to throw away repetitive terms which had gone stale, and thus to have the courage to change terminology. He taught me to ask questions, ironical questions. The other teacher I would like to mention here was Ernst Käsemann – I shall be visiting him this evening. I was always arguing with him, and of course that isn't difficult! But I found that very exciting and stimulating. I was terribly offended above all when he attacked Bultmann; here I was always on the side of the grandfather, not the father. Nevertheless he opened up to me much of the world within the New Testament.

I then had a typical woman's career, in other words none – at any rate in Germany. With every possible interruption and delay specific to women that one can think of, first children and then a return to the university, I was with great enthusiasm a student counsellor in a college and a teacher until finally for some years I became a professor in the United States, at Union Theological Seminary in New York. There I learned from two things above all: my encounter with the feminists and my encounter with the ecumenical world.

I want to say something else about another change in my theological thought, which really only happens to coincide with the year 1968. I am not one of the so called sixty-eighters; previously I had been thinking a bit about Auschwitz and its consequences, and was very aware of what was going wrong in the Western world. The number of starving children has not diminished in the last forty years, and during the 1960s we heard the term 'Third World' for the first time. We founded an ecumenical group in Cologne to which Marie Veit also belonged, and celebrated the 'Political Night Prayers', a new form of worship. For me that was a very eventful and splendid time. If I wanted to sum up its theological results in a single phrase, I would say that we drew the consequences of Auschwitz: we rethought our understanding of sin. We called that the 'politicization of conscience'. What separates me from God is not my sexuality or the fact that I have always already been rejected

24

– I can't cope with that kind of talk. What really separates me from God is the way in which I am destroying my grandchildren's water supply.

So I really exist in an ecopolitical context in which I am involved with my whole existence. I contribute to making even more children starve; and the International Monetary Fund contributes to seeing that they have no proper upbringing, and so on. That is the politicization of the conscience. What we really need forgiveness for, what we sing 'Kyrie eleison' for, is connected with our real world, and any abstraction of that into a merely private sinfulness seems to me to be false. This is a point on which I still hope – though perhaps this hope is quite illusory – that one day we can also get into dialogue with our fundamentalist cousins. Some time they, too, must understand what sin is and what we now really need forgiveness and learning to arise and take up our beds and walk for. And for me that would be a starting-point which makes it so evident that as it were the bourgeois narrowing to the individual alone or the Catholic narrowing to sexuality alone is really not enough.

In this context of the politicizing of the conscience there then arose what we three – I, Jürgen Moltmann, and Baptist Metz, whom I really should have mentioned first – called 'political theology'. I have meanwhile ceased to use the term altogether. I well remember the very day when I heard of a *teologia de la liberación* for the first time and so to speak the scales fell from my eyes. This was really what I had been looking for all the time. What I have learned from liberation theology is how to speak clearly of what the real issue is. I have found a better translation of the word salvation (*soteria*) than we had previously, since the old term always led into this individuality. I have found a wider horizon and – something else I must mention – the concept of the 'interlocutor', which has become one of the most important terms for me. A right theology needs people in the middle to communicate and ask questions, in other words complaining women, widows, and other uneducated people. I don't want to do any more theology without listening to the interlocutors or being clear about who they are.

The other main problem on which I have worked for a long time and with which of course I am not finished is connected with this. In what sense can we talk of God? Mustn't that be an atheistic language? Isn't God dead, as Nietzsche remarked? I've fought much over this, struggled, interrogated myself, even contradicted myself. I want to mention two things here. The first is negative and relates to a basic concept of classical theology, that of omnipotence, with which I cannot live. I regard it as a male delusion; one doesn't need to know much Freud to understand that here we have a projection of male wishes on to God. It took some thirty years for me to be able to say that so clearly. It has also become clear to me through the basic theme of history. I think that God was very small in Auschwitz; God had no friends at this time; God's sun, righteousness, did not shine; and the Spirit had no dwelling in our land. For me these are more precise descriptions of what it really means to talk of power.

Now, and this is the second thing, feminist theology came to my help here. One of its most important corrections, revisions which in my view are absolutely necessary, is not the exchange of pronouns. We can settle that in passing and it doesn't mean anything. What we really need to work on is a differentiated concept of power. I am not fond of using German terminology here, since the German word *Ermächtigung* has become loaded and has been destroyed in our language, at any rate for my generation. So let me use the English term 'empowerment'; this denotes that good power is what makes others powerful, empowers others, makes us capable of love. During my studies I never understood that as disciples of Jesus we can all cast out demons, and are to feed the hungry. That 'everything is possible' for us was also a recognition which dawned on me long after my studies. Only at a late stage did I come to realize how remote our prevailing christological and theological abstractions made us from real possibilities of realization, from real action and from the trust of Jesus in his brothers and sisters.

The concept of God needs to be revised, and the interlocutors who helped me here were above all the Jews with whom I was in dialogue. I am thinking above all of Hans Jonas, whom I met later, but I am also thinking of Emil Fackenheim, Elie Wiesel and other writers, whose corrections of traditional theology have helped me. This criticism of omnipotence, and an understanding of God which dispenses with omnipotence and a fixation on omnipotence, contains an element of feminine thought. It similarly attempts to think rather differently about the opposition between activity and passivity which is so deeply anchored in male sexuality and thus also in male dogmatics. These are topics which have passionately attracted me and concerned me, and which have drawn me increasingly into a mystical understanding of the knowledge of God from experience, as the scholastic definition puts it. That is perhaps my last possible change. By this I do not mean New Age and the like, but my mysticism, which is also lived out seriously in everyday life. I connect this with something that I would still like to write about, which I think is necessary for the conciliar process: the concept of resistance. I am attempting to democratize both concepts, those of mysticism and resistance, in order to remove their elitist connotations. A mystical theology for all is an indispensable postulate, as Karl Rahner saw. We are all mystics, as great mystics, men and women, have kept saying, and it has become increasingly important to me to understand and convey that.

What remains for us to do theologically for the future in the face of the final victory of capitalism, which now has no compulsion to show a human face within the Third World because there is no competition, is to develop a liberating theology which is orientated on these basic conceptions, the mystical presence of God and resistance. I believe that without these other theologies of liberation I would never have been so encouraged to go on hoping for a liberation of Europe as well.

Second Round

Johann Baptist Metz
Elisabeth Moltmann-Wendel
Norbert Greinacher

Johann Baptist Metz

That one has perhaps changed too much or too quickly is a suggestion that one hears not only in the censure of one's opponents but sometimes also in the praise of one's friends. That happens, for example, when my friend Jürgen Moltmann writes, 'Metz is always good for a surprise.' So here I do not want to talk about the ways in which I have changed – in any case I have often spoken about that – but, like Eberhard Jüngel before me, about the ways in which I have not changed. That is the only way in which I can risk saying something about those aspects of my life which still shape my theology without being arbitrary.

Towards the end of the Second World War, at the age of sixteen, I was snatched out of school and conscripted into the army. After a hasty training in the barracks at Würzburg I arrived at the front, which by that time had already advanced over the Rhine into Bavaria. My company consisted solely of young people, well over a hundred of them. One evening the company commander sent me with a message to battalion headquarters. I wandered during the night through shattered, burning villages and farmsteads, and when next morning I returned to my company I found only the dead: dead bodies, overwhelmed by a combined fighter-bomber and tank attack. I could only look into the still, dead faces of all those with whom on the previous days I had shared the anxieties of childhood and the joys of youth. I cannot remember anything but a silent cry. I can still see myself there today, and my childhood dreams have collapsed before that memory. A great gap had been torn in my powerful Bavarian Catholic socialization with its well-knit trust. What happens if one then does not go to a psychologist, but into the church, and if one cannot be talked out of such unreconciled experiences either by the church or by theology, but together with them wants to believe and together with them wants to talk about God?

The personal background that I have indicated here still stamps my theological work. For example, the category of danger still has a central role in it; I do not want to abandon the apocalyptic metaphors of the history of faith; I mistrust an ideology which has been smoothed over in an idealistic way. And above all, the whole of my theological work has been governed by a special sensitivity to theodicy, the question of God in the face of the history of the suffering of the world, 'his' world. What was later to be called 'political theology' has its roots here: talking of God in conversion to the passion. Those who speak of God as Jesus does, take into account the possibility of the destruction of their own pre-conceived certainties by the misfortune of others.

So I must now say something about political theology, for which I have stood, and which over the years has in many ways also associated me particularly with Jürgen Moltmann and Dorothee Sölle; it has associated me with them in a kind of indirect ecumenism, a solidarity in the public dispute over God and the world. Here are some reflections on the course of political theology.

1. My experiences of the so-called Paulusgesellschaft, which had already devoted itself to the dialogue between Christians and Marxists in the early 1960s, and then particularly of Ernst Bloch and the Frankfurt School, so to speak politicized me out of the existential and transcendental magic circle of theology. I really always understood the critical discussion with Marxism to be grappling with the dramatization of the theme of theodicy as a criticism of society. I did not want to spare politics and political culture this perspective of theodicy – as the various forms of pragmatism recommended

– but I did not want to express it in the same way as Marxism: namely always and unconditionally as a question of the suffering of the other, the suffering even of enemies, and as a question of past suffering, which no struggle of the living, however passionate, can reconcile. This fusion of politics and theodicy had and has a high price; it keeps making this political theology the laughing-stock of all political pragmatists and really also of all political utopians (outside Chrisitianity and within). But without this perspective of theodicy, how does one rescue political life from sheer political Darwinism, whether it is to be established directly in a straight line or in a protracted way through dialectic?

2. If I am right, the atmosphere of 1968, which is so reviled today, had one particular effect on me: it drove out of me the all too pliable theological talk of the historicity of faith and increasingly clearly confronted my theology with history itself, with that history which bears catastrophic names like Auschwitz. Time and again since then I have asked myself why our theology pays so little attention to such a catastrophe and to the history of human suffering. Have we perhaps used far too strong categories for the theological interpretation of history, which conceal all traumas far too hastily and stunt our sense of danger? Does theology really heal all wounds? Auschwitz acts as an ultimatum for me here. In the light of Auschwitz the supposedly 'weak' categories of memory and narrative, which can also express the terror of the logos of theology, along with attention to the anamnetic culture which is developed in Jewish history, play an every greater role for me.

3. Since the late 1960s there were two impulses from the Second Vatican Council in particular which I sought to defend and to reinforce under the slogan 'political theology'. First was the stimulus to walk upright in the church ('Only those who walk upright can also kneel of their own accord

and give thanks with joy') and the revision of my church's attitude to political enlightenment, the germ of which is indicated here. Then above all there was the movement taking shape in this council, from European monocentrism into a world church which was painfully torn apart in social terms and culturally polycentric. Here my encounters with friends in the international journal *Concilium* were particularly fruitful for me.

Whereas it became increasingly clear to me on my visits to the United States that there is also a simmering conflict of civilization within the Catholicism of the Western, the so-called First, World, namely the apparent alienation and dissociation between Roman Catholicism on the one hand and the religious and political traditions of the Anglo-Saxon world on the other, above all the growing incorporation of the non-Western world, what had previously been called the Third World, became a new theological challenge. It exposed the logos of theology to the social suffering and misery of the poor nations and also to the suffering of cultural and ethnic otherness in a world and a world church dominated by the West.

There are two comments among many that I might make. One relates to my experience with the work of my friends and colleagues in Latin America among the base communities. It seemed to me to be most impressive and really also most hopeful where it began completely 'from below', where all merely rhetorical radicalization of the message had failed, where a pious metaphysics stuck in one's throat, where one refused to try to put the speechless misery into words, and initially the only thing that counted was to be there. Presumably there is one element in the life of a base church which we do not (or no longer) have in a middle-class church, namely the way in which a social and cultural struggle for identity goes hand in hand with the construction and experience of religious identity. So much pain and risk is

34

attached to words like 'liberation' and 'base community' that I can only warn against any easy use of them here.

My second biographical comment is about the faces in America, particularly the faces of the Indios, faces which are marked by the dark shadows of what there is called the mysticism of the Andes. 'Mourning rains in the Andes', I wrote in the diary of my time there. There is nothing romantic about the mourning on the faces of the Indios. In my view the Indios find our Western civilization so difficult not so much because, as we like to say, they are 'under-developed', but primarily because they are different, and this otherness has mysteries which need to be respected. Do we have enough sensitivity to difference and otherness here at home to recognize and to save this otherness before it is finally wiped out by the rape of the planet by Western civilization?

Meanwhile I am attempting to formulate a theological scheme, now also in relation to other cultural worlds, which also takes account of the 'postmodern' suspicion of the undeniable dangers of universalist approaches and yet does not fall victim to a flat relativization of cultural worlds: emphasizing respect for and obedience towards the authority of those who suffer. For me this authority is the only authority in which the authority of the God who judges manifests itself in the world for all men and women.

Here I shall break off. The scarlet thread running through this biographical course may be taken to be the *memoria passionis*, the remembrance of the suffering of others as the basic category of Christian talk of God, and thus the question of theodicy taken up again in the conditions of our time and dramatized in a way which is critical of society. Moreover, this is a question which for me has not simply been silenced and settled by the Christian message of redemption. Everywhere it remains a cry which can be loud or can be silent. That has recently led me, for example, to ask Jürgen

Habermas in a friendly way whether it has really been proved that the primal sense of human language is understanding and not perhaps the cry. I have questions for God, the God of Abraham, Isaac and Jacob, the God of Jesus, for which I have a language, but no answers. And so I have made my own prayer: Why, God, suffering, why guilt? Why have you (and here I have adopted a phrase from Eberhard Jüngel's personal statement) taken no precautions against evil?

Much though my theology is stamped with all this, to end with I would like you to realize that I interpreted that unique teacher, Karl Rahner, who himself hardly spoke of theodicy and negative theology, in this perspective, because in talking about God like this I did not want to leave him out. In 1984, the year of his death, I wrote: 'Karl Rahner never interprets Christianity as the good conscience of advanced citizenship, never as a kind of middle-class domestic religion from which all fatally threatened hope and all vulnerable and refractory longing is driven out . . . Right through his work there continues to run this longing which I felt never to be sentimental, never to storm heaven, but to be more like the silent sighing of creation, like a wordless cry for light before the dark countenance of God.'

Elisabeth Moltmann-Wendel

I come from a family which was strongly influenced by the Confessing Church. My parents were active members from the time of its foundation. My father died in autumn 1934, not leaving us much apart from the conviction that a Christian had to oppose National Socialism. My mother held to this conviction, and went regularly to the Confessing Church Bible studies in Potsdam, which I really see as a kind of underground church. She always used to bring back political news, with which she fed us at breakfast time next day. My basic feeling as a child in the Third Reich was that we were different from the others, that we went against the grain and thought against the grain, but that there was a whole mass of people like us, whom I met within the church. They seemed to me to be courageous, spontaneous, independent and untroubled. When I was confirmed, I insisted on joining the Confessing Church; I got the 'red card' which, with the picture of Martin Niemöller, from now on was always in my purse. This was a mixture of icon and mascot, and always also gave me a feeling of security in my feeling of otherness. Another basic feeling also comes from this time: a mistrust of intact churches and their representatives. At that time the names were those of Bishops Marahrens, Meiser and Wurm. Nowadays the names are different.

I began to study theology in Berlin immediately after the end of the war, not because I wanted to become a theologian, but because the theological faculty was the first to begin lectures, as early as July 1945. However, after a semester of Hebrew and Greek I was so gripped by the subject that I decided to continue with it. That was not a revolution for women. In 1945 a third of the students in Berlin were women, and they were wiser and more experienced than the weary warriors who decided to study theology at that time.

After two years at the Kirchliche Hochschule in Berlin I succeeded in getting a permit for Göttingen. I had turned down a permit for Tübingen because Tübingen and its theology seemed to me to be too pious and too unpolitical. Thielicke's Good Friday sermons against the Stuttgart Declaration of Guilt had been given here, and that did not fit my Confessing Church tradition. At that time Göttingen was a Mecca for a theology which was critical of the churches and society. My teachers were Hans Joachim Iwand, Ernst Wolf and Otto Weber, who grappled intensively with the Nazi past both personally and theologically, and gave us theological foundations for an understanding of ourselves and the churches which was open to the world and the ecumene. In my view, the direction was set here for a Protestant political theology, though it took two decades for it to take shape. One of the three, Otto Weber, encouraged me – or rather he urged me, since I would not have thought myself capable of doing anything of the kind – to produce a dissertation on Hermann Friedrich Kohlbrügge, a Dutch theologian whose German pupils had taken very different political courses in the Third Reich: some into the Confessing Church and some into the German Christians.

I was the first 'virgin' – *virgo doctissima*, as the doctoral certificate put it – to gain a doctorate in the Protestant Theological Faculty in Göttingen, in 1951. I had been preceded by a married woman, who was called *domina doctissima*. But that also ended my theological career. For I got married, and in so doing according to the regulations of the time lost all my rights to train as an assistant pastor, to be ordained and to serve as a pastor. My generation did not protest against this, but succumbed to the sweet theological poison of the time, which suggested that equal clerical status also meant equal rights. And it also succumbed to the illusions cherished in German society and theology, of a partnership of equal grace, shared, complementary, communicating – as these were described in increasingly attractive terms by various theologians. But in the end HE, the man, was always the leading figure. He was the A, as Karl Barth put it, which comes before the B, the woman. It was a long time before we noted something that the feminist movement then made clear, that such a partnership is the sleeping pill of emancipation.

Over the next fifteen years I had four children and moved from place to place with my family: Berlin, Siegerland, Wuppertal, Bonn, Tübingen, the USA. (I very soon noticed how my intellectual and theological capacities and interests were growing weaker.) In the evening I was too exhausted after housework and looking after the children to provide intellectual company for my husband. In the first period of our marriage he had still shown me what he wrote, sermons and lectures, for critical comments. That soon stopped, presumably because I could no longer make any comment on them and also because I was far too tired. I also noticed that former fellow students now valued me in a friendly way at most as a wife and mother. My own history had virtually been wiped out. Above all it became clear to me that while in the meantime theology had discovered the workers and the social world, it had also come upon the psyche, and that led to new and fascinating theological schemes into which women in particular were also throwing themselves with verve, while the world of housework and the world of women remained undiscovered and irrelevant for theology. My existence and my theology no longer had any points of contact.

However, when the children grew older and light began to dawn, I noticed with delight that something was going on outside the limits of German theology which made me prick up my ears. At the World Council of Churches conference in Uppsala in 1968 there was talk of human rights. I had not previously come across that in the German context, but human rights concerned individuals, and therefore also women. Moreover people talked there of partnership, and this partnership was not profoundly German and Barthian, but very Anglo-Saxon: partnership as a dynamic process and a partnership of equals. When I heard the voice of Philip Potter on the radio in this connection it seemed to me to be the voice of an angel from heaven.

Another important experience was a visit by James Cone, the Afro-American liberation theologian. He made liberation theology, with its quite different approach, clear to me: beginning with human experience which is not limited to that of the dominant white male stratum.

A third experience for me was the student movement in 1968. Suddenly theologians were sitting in our living room who no longer wanted to discuss the Trinity, theodicy and the baptism of infants, but grass-roots democracy, monopolistic state capitalism, the imperative mandate. Theology had become somewhat earthy.

When I finally got hold of books and papers from the American, theological women's movement through American friends at the beginning of the 1970s, and when on a visit to the USA I saw that here was a different kind of theological and social thought which began with women, the world in which I had lived for more than forty years took a complete U-turn. I was myself, I was somebody, I no longer had to see myself in the function of mother and wife – and I began to write. First of all I worked on our German, Christian history of women over the past century, which had constantly been dominated by the notion of order rather than of human rights. The title of my first book in this sphere was *Human Rights for Women*. This brought me from my private sphere into the public world, where at first I had difficulty in expressing myself and developing my self-awareness. Here the great acceptance which I experienced from German women helped me. I also received help from the interest of some media, and in this connection I want to mention the *Evangelische Kommentare* and Hans Norbert Janowski, at that time their editor. Not least I was helped by the interest and curiosity of my husband in questions which had previously been unknown in the theological sphere.

Over subsequent years I attempted to develop feminist theology in company with other women, the theology which begins from the social experiences of women within a sexist society and which investigates all theological thought, even standing it on its head. For me personally these were the experiences of a middle-class woman who had lost her person and her identity. In addition there were now quite different women's experiences, of being selfless without a self, very varied experiences of economic exploitation (the low-paid groups), of violence, incest and sexual exploitation. In addition there were the experiences of women in the ecumenical movement, prostitution, sex tourism, the loss of their own culture as a result of male, white theology, colonial exploitation and the dominance of Western feminist approaches.

How can women coming from such experiences, which are never mentioned or recognized by theology, be liberated? Where does the message of the love of God and being a child of God find its place and its expression here?

At that time I wrote a book, in English entitled *The Women around Jesus*, which was widely read. For many women it showed the way forward. It was about ceasing to be governed by others, no longer being content with a derived identity (instead of one's own), and determining one's own life despite or precisely in all the wounds and hurts. One more thing which women had hardly learned, and which causes profound terror to most male theologians and

churchmen, was self-love. Psychology had long since discovered that this was necessary for becoming human. It was
regularly practised on the margins of the church in therapies,
but at the centre of the church it was still regarded as – in
Calvin's words – 'the most harmful pestilence', although it
derives directly from the gospel: love your neighbour(s) as
yourself. At present a globalizing and generalizing understanding of sin dominates public theology and preaching and
makes it loveless and bodiless.

Feminist theology opens up a new place from which
theology is done, and it has found a firm place at the grass
roots, in academies and at Kirchentage. For me it raises no
claim to absoluteness, but it does raise a claim to be heard.
Sometimes its results can evoke a primal male anxiety. The
inability of many Christians to think in differences instead of
dualisms makes it difficult for them to find access to other
patterns of thought which are important for life. Even now
many theologians are characterized by an 'either-or' way of
thinking, and church governments are more concerned about
unity than about the truth. It seems to me that a religious
claim to absoluteness still has hold of the brain and heart of
theology, and is passing over the new challenges.

That also explains the mistrust of German theological
institutions, faculties and church governments, which give
few opportunities to feminist theology and women working
in this sphere (the situation is different in many Western
countries and also in Asia and Africa). In Germany, the
country which is richest in different theologies, for a variety
of reasons there is a strange unanimity in excluding feminist
theology from theological discourse.

Internationally, feminist theology has produced a wealth
of theological research over the last twenty years. To mention
just a few areas: there is the rediscovery of women's
traditions in the Old and New Testaments, in theology and
church history; other hermeneutical approaches to the Bible

have been opened up; in systematic theology women have introduced alternative, non-authoritarian interpretations of justification, grace, life, images of God and christology. A new concept of rationality, in which feeling and experience are no longer split off, is developing.

I personally have felt it important over the last ten years to develop a theology of the body. At a very early stage the analysis of the American theologian Rosemary Ruether became important for me. This demonstrates the tragic break between the holistic Jewish and Christian way of thinking and dualistic Greek and Aristotelian thought. Here began the development within which the body was opposed to the spirit and in which man was given the spirit and woman the body. I wanted to start here to revive a theology orientated on women and the body.

For me a theology of corporeality has three topical aspects:

1. An anthropological aspect, which begins with human beings in their wholeness and not in their sinfulness.

2. A cosmic aspect, which also sees the macrocosm of creation in the microcosm of the body and does not make the cosmos an object again in a much-quoted concern for the creation. As R.zur Lippe put it, 'We must heal ourselves in order to become bearable to the creation again.'

3. A social aspect. According to United Nations reports, human dignity is today being threatened in the body: by hunger, torture and poverty. In addition, as has been evident at the latest since the World Women's Conference in Peking, women's dignity is threatened by sexual violence and rape. The women's conference in Costa Rica in 1993 therefore called for a deconstruction of the theologies of the spirit which disparage physical life. There was a demand, in their place, for discussion of corporeality in theology, since the resurrection was a reality in present-day life.

In these statements, along with other women of Christianity, I find an expression of my theological concern.

43

Here the frontiers of a feminist theology which is merely partisan open up on a theology which is orientated on the body and the life of all.

Norbert Greinacher

I come from a home which was deeply stamped by the 'Catholic milieu'. My home was ultra-conservative, the most conservative imaginable. My father, one of seventeen brothers and sisters who lived in a village, was taught in Latin by the village pastor – along with Wendelin Rauch, who later became an archbishop – so that he could make the jump to the Catholic boys' seminary in Constance. For years my grandfather on my mother's side – a successful middle-class businessman – was a Centre Party delegate to the Baden Landstag. My grandmother on my mother's side was the first woman in the Freiburg district council – of course as a Centre Party delegate.

My parents – I was the youngest of five daughters and sons – never influenced me directly to become a priest. But I remember that they were very pleased when, as the youngest member of the family, I told them on leaving school that I intended to enter the theological seminary in Freiburg.

I have vivid memories of my studies – first at the Catholic Theological Faculty of the University of Freiburg – although they now lie forty-six years in the past. I was impressed above all by Martin Heidegger, to whom I listened for four semesters, though that was forbidden: for example his series of lectures on 'What does it mean to think?' After the lecture I had to run back to the Collegium Borromaeum to be there in time for supper. I suppose that the then Director, Fr Schlund, knew why I was out of breath at the common meal, but he evidently tolerated it. Nowadays I am more sceptical about my former teacher Heidegger and his 'disciple' Bernhard Welte, to whom I then listened with veneration.

A year of studies at the Institut Catholique in Paris in 1952/53 was a breakthrough in my personal theological development. By a stroke of good fortune I was given a scholarship – along with my friend Bernard Adler – to this Catholic private university. For me it was an improbable opening up of the 'Catholic milieu' of Freiburg Catholicism to the light of the wider world.

It was an opening up in two respects. On the one hand I discovered that there was 'another' theology; above all I was influenced by the lectures of my teacher Daniélou, who reported the most recent 'Qumran' discoveries to us in a very lively way. I repeat, this was 1952! On the other hand, through another stroke of good fortune I came into lively contact with a whole series of worker priests and with the 'Mission de France', above all with my late friend Yvan Daniel, who had written the book *France – Pays de Mission?* This encounter with theologians and worker priests left a deep mark on my life.

My appointment to the editorial committee of the international theological journal *Concilium* in 1969 was also important for me. I learned much in the twenty-five years of my membership, which was ended in 1994 by a conflict which deeply wounded me. During this period I gained an extraordinary number of new insights and new experiences at the annual General Meetings and in personal contact with the friends who have shaped my biography. Above all I should mention that without meeting Leonardo Boff and Gustavo Gutiérrez personally on the editorial committee of *Concilium* I would never have had such a deep personal involvement in liberation theology and the experiences of the churches in Latin America. This was an encounter which was of decisive significance for my life, my faith and my theology.

The horizons of my life and thought also opened up as a result of my years as academic assistant in the Catholic Theological Faculty in Vienna to my unforgettable late teacher and friend Ferdinand Klostermann. As early as 1963 he had asked my bishop, Bishop Schäufele, to release me to accept this post with a view to gaining the Habilitation, the qualification for university teaching. Schäufele said no, so I became a pastor in Badenweiler in the Black Forest – not the worst time of my life.

Schäufele and Klostermann met literally on the steps of St Peter's in Rome during the Second Vatican Council, at which Klostermann was a *peritus*. Klostermann again asked Schäufele whether he might release Greinacher with a view to post-doctoral studies. Schäufele immediately gave his permission, remarking that he had probably done Greinacher an injustice.

The time in Vienna, between 1965 and 1966, was very important for me. On the one hand I got to know my later friends Otto Maur (a university pastor and founder of the 'Galerie nächst Stephan') and Karl Strobel (a student pastor), to both of whom I owe a great deal. On the other hand I came into contact with many theologians and friends in the former German Democratic Republic, in what was then Yugoslavia, and in Poland and Hungary. This broadened my horizons to an extraordinary degree. However, I find it frightening that these varied contacts virtually died out after the revolution in 1989 – despite many efforts on my part.

The time I spent at the Catholic Theological Faculty of the University of Münster was also important to me. I taught there for five semesters, and the friendly relations with Karl Rahner, Johann Baptist Metz, Walter Kasper and Karl Lehmann were of great significance.

The link with Leonardo Boff and Gustavo Gutierrez through *Concilium*, which I have already mentioned, together with my encounter with Johann Baptist Metz and – initially on the basis of his publications – with Jürgen Moltmann, represented a decisive theological turning point for me. I recognized that one cannot preach about freedom, equality, brotherhood and sisterhood, justice and subsidiarity from the pulpit on Sunday without working on Monday for more justice in our political society. So I also attempted to engage in politics to the best of my ability: as a co-founder of the August Bebel Group, as a member of the Social Democratic Party of Germany, by joining the blockade of the Cruise missile base in Mutlangen, and so on.

In my view, liberation theology presented itself as an authentic response of Christian faith to the inhuman situation of most men and women in Latin America. Many journeys to Latin America confirmed me in this view. On the one hand I was constantly shaken by the inhuman situation of poverty in the slums of Sao Paulo, in the country districts of Guatemala, in the suburbs of Lima in Peru, and elsewhere. I wanted to give an example of solidarity – along with Henning Scherf and others – by taking part in the coffee harvest in Nicaragua. My last excursion to Latin America with a party of seventeen in September 1995, to Mexico and Guatemala, was meant on the one hand to be a sign of solidarity with the Christians there. On the other hand I got the impression that those who took part in the visit gained experiences which they will never forget.

The Catholic Theological Faculty of Ellwangen was transferred to Tübingen in 1817 'to achieve more tolerance and to smooth out the confessional corners' (thus King Wilhelm I of Württemberg). According to legend, the Catholic professors of theology were the first Catholics in the city of Tübingen. I experienced this ecumenical breadth when I was called to Tübingen on 1 November 1969. Since that date I have lived, worked and taught in Tübingen. This ecumenical link also found architectural expression when, under the influence of Herr Lembke, the chief university architect, and not without my personal involvement – I was the delegate from my faculty responsible for buildings – in 1989 the libraries of the two faculties were combined in what I think to be an

48

aesthetically very beautiful and also very practical octagon. At that time, Herr Lembke said to me, 'It's necessary to enforce ecumenism through architectural structures'.

I also want to mention in this connection the 'Theological-Philosophical Working Group' in which for around twenty years, along with my Protestant colleague Professor Dr Dieter Rössler and my Catholic colleague Professor Dr Georg Wieland, about a dozen academic assistants, doctoral and post-doctoral students have gathered in my home in ecumenical fellowship for scholarly discussion. At the same time I would also like to refer to the Ecumenical Working Group, which meets about every four weeks for ecumenical dialogue during the academic year.

In recent years the prophetic dimension of Christian faith and Christian theology has become increasingly important for my theological thought. Here I do not understand prophets in the conventional way, as those who predict the future, but rather as those who pass critical judgment on the present situation from the roots of the Jewish and Christian traditions and who say what is to be done 'here and now'. I have the impression that this prophetic dimension of Christian faith has been increasingly lost in church and theology, although for example I Corinthians says: 'And God has appointed in the church first apostles, second prophets and third teachers' (12.28).

It is essential for the church once again to listen to contemporary prophets: for example to Bishop Gaillot in France, to Bishop Ruiz in Mexico, to the recently deceased Bishop Hypolito in Brazil, to pastors like Heinz Schulz in the area around Frankfurt station and to theologians like Tissa Balasuriya in Sri Lanka, to mention just a few.

In my childhood and my youth, and as a rising priest and theologian, I accepted the Christian faith, the authority of the church and the structure of Catholic scholastic theology without question, and they gave me support and security.

However, gradually question upon question arose, above all the question of theodicy. This question has intensified for me personally when – time and again – with a dozen of my students I have held a mini-seminar at the Liebenau Foundation, a church foundation near Ravensburg in the Swabian uplands, which offers a home to around 2,000 handicapped people. I spent a day, along with all my students, from eight in the morning until eight in the evening, in a group with ten of the most seriously handicapped. They were physically and mentally handicapped, and I could not carry on even the simplest rational conversation with them. This was partly because they could not speak, but even more because what passed through their lips was incomprehensible or totally confused. This raised the question of the meaning or meaninglessness of life for me and my students in a terrifying way.

When my late friend Walter Dirks, a committed Catholic journalist, visited his friend Romano Guardini, one of the most significant Catholic theologians of this century, on his deathbed, Guardini said to him: 'I am ready to go before God's judgment seat and to let him ask me about my life. I have sinned, and I will give an account of that to God. But then I shall also have questions to put to God, and I shall insist on an answer, for example to the problem of the fate of innocent children who suffer.'

This is a paradox by all our usual norms: the accused questioning the judge!

European Christians raised the question of the meaning or meaninglessness of human life above all in connection with the Lisbon earthquake of 1 November 1755. Nowadays we can hardly imagine the mental and spiritual shock caused to Western Christianity when in a few minutes the city of Lisbon fell in rubble and ashes and around 60,000 people were killed. The established order of the Christian West was shaken. A decisive blow was dealt to faith in divine providence and in the rationality of the world. The optimism of the Enlightenment collapsed. Only five years before the Lisbon catastrophe, in 1750, Jean Jacques Rousseau had written his *Discours sur les arts et les sciences*, in which he described the primal cultural state of humankind as the happiest; this led to the slogan 'return to nature' among his contemporaries. And years before, in 1697, the German philosopher Gotthold Wilhelm Leibniz was in correspondence with Queen Sophie Charlotte of Prussia. In this correspondence Leibniz used the term 'theodicy' for the first time in connection with Romans 3.5, and thus coined a phrase which has influenced theological discussion decisively down to the present day. How can the notion of a God who is benevolent towards human beings be reconciled with the notion of the justice of God? After Lisbon Voltaire raised the questions: What crime, what sins had those children committed who were torn bloodily from their mothers' wombs? Was Lisbon, which perished, more full of vice than London and Paris, which were luxuriating in pleasure? 'Lisbon has been swallowed up by the abyss and Paris is dancing.'

This question of God's justice has become even more acute after the Holocaust, to which six million people fell victim.

But I personally have above all been shaken once again by the fact that in the sixteenth century, in the name of the church, around eighty million Indios were annihilated. Tzvetan Todorov writes: 'The sixteenth century was to witness the greatest genocide in human history.'

My theology of unquestioning certainty has increasingly become a theology of doubt. Here I comfort myself with the remark in the Gospel of Matthew that after the resurrection of Jesus the eleven disciples withdrew to Galilee, to the mountain to which Jesus had directed them. 'And when they saw him they worshipped him; but some doubted' (28.16 f.).

Third Round

Jörg Zink
Philip Potter
Hans Küng

Jörg Zink

The beginnings of my theological career now lie precisely fifty years in the past, here in Tübingen in the winter semester of 1945/46. We returned then from five years of war and imprisonment and wanted to hear whether theology could give us new ground under our feet after the great invasion of all our intellectual foundations. I shall talk about this time not as an academic theologian, but as an everyday Christian, who has been surrounded by everyday people all his life.

At that time we needed a theology which was formulated in this great period of upheaval, and the beginnings of such a theology could be detected. But on the whole what we were offered came from the 1920s. On the one hand this was an authoritative theology of the Word which offered firm material to those returning home who were hungry for orientation, and at any rate stated the issue clearly. On the other hand there was the beginning of the debate on the demythologizing of the New Testament, in which we developed our theological self-awareness. And since in our youth we could not learn to respect the convictions of others, the dispute between Barthians and Bultmannians – and also pietists – became a kind of continuation of the war with other means. It dominated our study. But as I myself hated the war, I soon withdrew from the dispute into my own discoveries. Later we also got Dietrich Bonhoeffer as the example of the process of testing that made us theologians. At that time Bonhoeffer was the great excuse for the church and theology, which was meant to show that we had offered resistance. And at that time an influence which shaped me was the memory of a simple pastor, a pious pietist, who had given me the beginnings of a spirituality in prison. I wanted to be someone like him.

Nowadays I ask myself above all what we didn't learn at that time, what was avoided. We were taught that there was no point in getting to know other religions. All truth was assembled in Christianity. We were taught that myth was an obsolete way of thinking. So we were not interested in any early forms of piety. It was clear that the pastors didn't need any knowledge of depth psychology. A teacher who recommended that we should read Jung was openly mocked. Anything like personal experience could be dispensed with. We regarded it as a kind of turning inwards which was inappropriate for a theologian. Despite admirable lectures on church history, history was thought to be unimportant, because all salvation was to be found in the decision of faith in the present moment. Only rarely and timidly were lines of influence drawn from theology to political and social questions. Even the original beginnings of a political theology, like that of Helmut Thielicke, were soon diverted under the pressure of an overall conservative approach at the beginning of the Cold War. It is also amazing that questions like how wars could be avoided in the future, or the shape of peace, were reflected on only in small theological circles, like the Swabian society, but hardly at all in the faculties. And that was at a time when the victims of the war were sitting at lectures with crutches and Braille equipment. Be this as it may, anyone who is one of only three out of four hundred fellow airmen to survive the war has to consider what the question of peace requires of him.

And above all, there was virtually no critical discussion of National Socialism, which at that time only seemed to be dead, rather than being really dead. It should have called for a kind of confession of sins from all too many of our teachers. The atmosphere was one of a perplexed restoration, of people who would much have preferred to go on as though nothing had happened. And so all in all, in 1950, after our studies, we had the worst preparation imaginable for facing the challenges of the second half of the century.

I need to say how I have changed from this point on. Changes in a person have many aspects, For example: what has been reinforced in the course of fifty years? What new insights have there been? What has one left behind? In what is one still alone? Where in the end has one found oneself back at one's beginnings? Where has one remained the same? What small beginnings have perhaps become more credible? What does one expect today? I shall go briefly through this series of questions. It is appropriate material for a self-examination by someone who has passed the age of seventy.

What has been reinforced? First of all, the need for involvement in politics. It was a logical and straight line from the religious socialism of my parents through the demonstrations against the rearmament of West Germany around 1950 to the peace movement, the occupations and human chains of the 1980s. My own personal beginning lay in the war, during which in prison I met a French resistance fighter, a fellow-prisoner who was facing execution. This noble, sensitive and unyielding figure cured me at that time of nationalistic obscurantism and showed me what resistance against injustice had to look like and what it might make of a person.

So for me the discovery of a political theology in the 1960s was a liberation. When Dorothee Sölle and Johann Baptist Metz made the move from an existential or transcendental hermeneutic to a political hermeneutic, at last one could approach conditions in society from a theological perspective Unfortunately the significance of this shift has only dawned on the churches after the usual twenty-year time-lag. It came so late that in 1980 I left the service of the church – with the friendly consent of my grateful superiors – in order to be able to speak seriously for the peace and ecological movements.

For I also needed this freedom in that field. When in 1965 I presented two films about 'The Destruction of Creation' on television, my church authority thought that I should turn to theological questions. I should leave this topic to the state and the business world. Note that these people were not bad theologians; but they were children of the kind of theology that was to be learned after the war, for which interest in the first article of faith had been condensed into a dispute over what was called 'natural theology'.

The kind of creation spirituality that can be found today, say, in Moltmann, in a quite different form in Matthew Fox, or yet again in feminism, will continue to occupy us as a domestic task well into the new century. A theology which knows nothing but the lonely family history or family tragedy between God and humankind is a thing of the past. Here we shall probably again also go through the long-forgotten notion of the cosmic Christ; we shall also certainly need it if our dialogue with other religions is to be given a theological answer.

I have observed one of the steps taken by theology, i.e. liberation theology, only from afar. Throughout my work I have failed to escape the provincial framework of Germany and its environs, whereas my contemporaries have long since been in orbit around the earth. But what has made a great mark on me has been the feminist wing of liberation theology. Already as a schoolboy in the 1930s I had to go into a bookshop and collect *The Woman's World* for my mother. Of course I also read it, and thus got to know the great women who stood behind this paper. And when I was fifteen, my mother told me about the secret woman which every right man has inside him and whom he must not allow to starve. This has made me take sensuality very much to heart, a sensuality which has become increasingly suspect to males; it is in this connection that I understand the quest for corporeality which is Elisabeth Moltmann's concern. Since then I have constantly had a grim enjoyment in observing how there is still a childish anxiety about women also among men in the church.

What else has been reinforced? In 1946 I concelebrated a eucharist in a Catholic monastery with an Orthodox bishop, a Catholic abbot and the head of the chancery of the Evangelical Church in Germany, Hans Asmussen. Since then I have never succeeded in maintaining any kind of confessional bond. And I think that today we are going beyond the fringes of our archaic consciousness, happily and unconcerned, wherever the remains of the confessional walls lie around the landscape like mediaeval stone circles. I keep celebrating the eucharist somewhere with one Catholic priest or another. For the confessions are deader than they give themselves out to be, and it is now high time to envisage in all freedom a pan-Christian council – albeit a formal one and thus one without prospects – after the by now long-standing suggestions of Yves Congar, Heinrich Fries or Karl Rahner, rather than waiting until one day the Spirit of God drives it into our heads that we have failed to recognize what will serve our peace.

Over the last thirty-five years a certain distancing from the language of Canaan has not so much changed as intensified in me, since I have been attempting to breathe life into the biblical text with a good deal of imagination because of the alienation which young people feel from the Bible. At that time I told myself, 'There must be music in these texts.' That is more important than fidelity to ancient sentence-structures. I would do it today with even greater freedom.

Over this period my lack of interest in theological disputes has also intensified. I have been accused of almost everything by my dear brothers in office. Hardly a single hostile stereotype of the West German middle-class ideology has been left out. However, I have proved to myself the twofold maxim that one should immediately accept any offer of dialogue, but not react to any attacks below the belt. Not even to the most recent one, that I am an anti-Judaist. On each occasion I have said my piece and left it to my audience to make up their minds about it. I wanted to disaccustom myself from disputes. I cannot see anything in the *rabies theologorum* which could serve truth. I wish that we could have a theology and a church in which we could speak freely and openly about all the things that are notoriously unclear to us all, and that means the whole field of theology. I would like a dialogue in which the prime concern was not to seek out errors, but in which unaccustomed statements were allowed to stand, including some which, while false by previous standards, could one day reveal themselves as true. I regard the desire of theologians to be right as the only real heresy.

What new insights have there been? I see the rediscovery of eschatology by the friend whom we are celebrating today as an important step which has really brought us something new. It has freed us from the narrow-gauge eschatology of our student days. Since it appeared, it has been permissible once again to look into the future, to expect salvation from the future and to bring about something like salvation on this earth.

After that, another new discovery which I had was the end of self-righteous criticism in theology. I think that it is time to deal with other religions more honourably and more cautiously than before. Hans Küng has told us much here. Our goal must be an inter-religious, ecumenical theology. To discover that, as Paul Tillich already urged, we shall have to develop a systematic theology which is structured throughout by the wealth of problems and facts in the study of religion, and which identifies tasks to be achieved in bringing order to dialogue with other religions.

What have I left behind? The first thing that I left behind was Karl Barth's *Church Dogmatics*. After about 8,000 pages of fascinating reading I came to roughly the conclusion that Eberhard Jüngel has recently stated in the *Zürcher Zeitung*: the truth cannot be as long as that. It is now already forty years since I parted company with Barth, with great gratitude.

The second was a legacy of the Lutheran doctrine of the two kingdoms. I told myself: if I am living as a democrat in a country with an approximately democratic constitution, then I cannot possible look as reverentially on a secular authority as one could in the times of princes and kings. At an early stage I felt that this theological idol was running after us with an iron-grey beard. Didn't we have to attempt to weave together organically all the forces in this society, including state and church? And in the five hundred years of our church hadn't this disastrous doctrine of two kingdoms failed to be of service to any particular state with all its heart and all its soul and all its strength? And isn't that clearly expressed down to the present day in the reactionary state-church law of our country?

What did I have to discover for myself? Forty years ago I experienced the reshaping of hermeneutics with Gerhard Ebeling. Or with Ernst Käsemann. Or with Ernst Fuchs, who with his 1954 *Hermeneutics* stimulated us to render Pauline texts in the everyday language of today. Something to be learned from Fuchs was that I am responsible not only for what I say but also for the state in which my word arrives in the ears of my hearers.

However, what I always missed was a concern for the relations between word and image. For hermeneutics is in fact a preoccupation not just with the word, but above all also with human imagery. The image stands for the reality that the word means, and I have in fact translated it only if my word has aroused notions in a contemporary man or woman which come close to the notions of an ancient writer. So what was someone who was to spend his life making television, i.e. selling the word as a series of images, to do, as long as theology had hardly made a start on a hermeneutics of the image? In this connection, time and again I also missed a wider theology of the beautiful, for which as a rule we at most reserve a standing place at the back.

Is there something that in my old age takes me back to my beginnings? Yes there is, and it is doing so with increasing power. It is the topic of mysticism. Already as a child and as a young man I had intense mystic experiences, and since then I have always suffered under the casual way in which our theology has brushed aside religious experience, religious immediacy and with it everything mystical. At the age of twenty I wrote home from the war: 'Unless Christianity rediscovers its mystical background, then it no longer has anything to say to us.' After more than fifty years I firmly stand by this statement. Unfortunately over long periods of my life I imposed on myself the prohibition which was instilled into us as students against interpreting the Christian faith in mystical terms. Today I am beginning to speak more clearly of this shift of our proclamation into the metaphorical language of mysticism, which is stamped by experience and immediacy, by sensuality and a readiness for action.

What could be regained by a rediscovery of the mystical tradition? First of all a new look at biblical mysticism, which for a long time has been suppressed, but which is in fact present in many facets. But also a deeper spirituality which we Protestants so lack. We could expand our one-sidedly theistic image of God. We could part company with an age-old Christian dualism. We could also discover the social and political energy which has always stemmed from mysticism.

We would discover a new language for our discussion with the modern sciences. We could also gain material for building bridges between the confessions. Finally we would also find a new courage for the prophetic ministry of the church. For mysticism and prophecy are certainly not opposites, but rather stem from one another.

At all events, I hope that here, as in other matters, there will come a time when the right half of the brain has become more for theologians than simply a dried plum.

My most important teacher before 1950 was Romano Guardini. As a Protestant theologian I gladly acknowledge that my decisive teacher was a Catholic.

What has not changed in me? Most things, I hope, and I hope that on the whole I have remained myself. I have found it worthwhile in theological discussion over fifty years to pass over at least every other fashion in a friendly way and only to share the views of the time when they agreed with my own convictions. For example, one does not survive fifty years of being a journalist on the great open-air stage if every ten years one appears to be someone else, but only if one remains recognizably the same throughout this whole period. For any jumping on to the bandwagon of fashionable views is always also a betrayal of one's own task.

The decisive closing question. Has one thing or another in me changed a little for the better? I may cautiously hope so.

I was always an impatient person. I could never bear it if a theologian wasted his years with sleep. A small plant of patience has perhaps thrived in the meantime.

I was always a loner. I have never believed in committees. I always felt that if something did not occur to one, it would not occur to one in a committee either. Today I can see how much imagination others have used which could also have been useful to me. And friendship takes the weight of the years off me.

I always wanted the whole of theology and the whole of a form of work for the church. Today I think that we are never responsible for a whole, not even for the whole truth, but always only for the partial truth which is entrusted to us today. A very little modesty in old age is nothing to be ashamed of.

Today I also think that there are things that are more important than understanding. As a young man I read on the wall in my school hall, *Sapere aude*. Dare it knowingly. Today I would write underneath it: 'Don't take your knowledge so seriously: the love of God is more important.'

For fifty years I have spoken, written and demonstrated for peace. Perhaps in so doing I myself have also become a little more peaceable.

I have struggled all my life for the preservation of creation. Today I wish I could still achieve something like a plant life, the life of a plant which is threatened with extinction but is protected. And after the end of eternal talking, above all to be in conversation with trees and beetles. In other words, to change myself from someone who works at a desk, not precisely into a potted plant, but at least into some wild shrub.

And that while I am losing confidence that life on this earth can still be saved. And while for me the future is taking on increasingly apocalyptic features.

At all events, it is very unclear what the future will bring and what it will ask of us. We will not be able to live on the basis of our reflections so far. The future is open, and is not suited to self-righteous prognoses. For ways which lead into the future are never there before us as ways. They only become ways as we travel them.

Philip Potter

It is a privilege and pleasure for me to congratulate you, Jürgen, on attaining the biblical age of seventy. I heartily welcome you to the 70s club, and assure you that it is great fun to be free to choose how to live and work, and to be more irreverent in what we say and write, especially as we have learned so much from you in your writings and presence in so many countries.

At this symposium we have been asked to share our experience and movements of thoughts during thirty or more years up to now, and to indicate what we perceive as open questions which preoccupy us. I am the odd man out here, because I am the only Third World person in this distinguished panel and I cannot claim to be an academic theologian. Nor have I written much. However, as a student of theology and history, and as a pastor and a participant in the international ecumenical movement for nearly fifty years, of which almost forty years have been spent in Europe, I have been exposed to the theological currents of this eventful period.

Let me first situate myself. I come from the Caribbean, which was the first area of the world, outside of the Mediterranean and the Near East, which was brutally occupied by Europe just over 500 years ago. We Caribbean folk are the most racially and culturally mixed people of the world – with the aborigines originating from Mongolia, with slaves brought over from many tribes in West and Central Africa, with Europeans of all sorts and with Jews coming from Europe to a more congenial environment, and later with Indians, Indonesians and Chinese being brought in as indentured labourers, and yet later with quite a few Syrians and Lebanese coming as peddlers and then as prosperous merchants. The Christian church in its various forms has been among us for nearly 500 years. The fundamental question posed by this encounter of so many different peoples in such different circumstances has been and remains how we regard and live with 'the other', made in the image of God.

When I became a theological student in 1944, I had the good fortune of being trained with others belonging to several churches of the Reformation. So it was an exercise in ecumenical learning. Immediately on my arrival in Jamaica, I joined the Student Christian Movement, and was made its study secretary. The most important thing I learned from the SCM was expressed in the famous slogan: 'We must have the Bible in one hand and the newspaper in the other hand.' It was explained that the newspaper, which dealt with the realities of our world, did not make sense without the message of the Bible as an historical book. And the Bible without the newspaper did not convey much relevance for today. This was tested by the fact that I was soon appointed as a secretary of the Jamaica Youth Movement, which was chiefly concerned about the struggle for political independence. Actually, this was not new to me because I was confirmed as a member of the church in January 1932, and in October 1932, at the first conference of political leaders calling for independence from colonial rule, I carried, as an eleven-year-old lad, in the main procession, a banner with the slogan: 'No taxation without representation.' I have, therefore, been guided by the fact that the text of the biblical record must be wrestled with in the context of the history of the people of Israel and of the early church, of the history of the church through the centuries, and of the history and actualities of our world. This has been my critical hermeneutical standpoint, having lived for seventy-

66

five years in what an historian has recently called 'the century of extremes'.

Except for four valuable years of pastorate in Haiti (1950–1954), my ministry until my retirement has been in the ecumenical movement, especially the World Student Christian Federation and the World Council of Churches. In the 1940s to 1960s there were many giants writing biblical and systematic theologies, like Eichrodt and von Rad, Bultmann, Jeremias and Käsemann, Barth, Brunner, Tillich and the Niebuhr brothers. Several of us younger persons decided that doing theology would mean for us enabling some things to be done for the renewal, mission and unity of the church, for human dignity and solidarity, and for justice, peace and a sustainable environment. That has in fact been my preoccupation for over forty years.

I want to raise some questions about the four major areas in which I have been engaged over the years: youth and student work; mission and evangelism; my period as General Secretary of the World Council of Churches: and my lifelong concern for socio-economic justice.

Youth and Students. I was associated with youth and student work in various capacities from 1948 to 1968 through the World Student Christian Federation and the World Council of Churches. At the inaugural Assembly of the WCC at Amsterdam in 1948, there were 100 of us as youth delegates, mostly students. Our first witness was that we were 50 women and 50 men – a pioneering effort which was going to be one of my main theological concerns, and in practice working for a true community of women and men in church and society. At that time, there was a tendency to speak about youth as the church of the future. We insisted that we were the church of today. At the second Assembly of the WCC in 1954, one of the major subjects was the laity – *laos*, the whole people of God. The Assembly was reminded that the laity represented 99% of the membership of the church. As young people we pledged ourselves to be the loyal opposition in the church, promoting the full participation of the whole people of God in all the aspects of the life of the church for the sake of its witness to the world.

Of course, in the 1950s it was not easy for youth and students in the West or East because of the fierceness of the Cold War. Youth were described as the silent, cautious generation, and in Germany they were credited as saying, '*ohne mich*', 'Count me out.' Youth and student work was just being developed in other continents under difficult circumstances. We talked then of the acceleration of history, but confessed our inability to comprehend it adequately, and speak and act prophetically about it within the church and in the world.

Our activities among youth and students included intensive Bible studies related to the issues of church and society, leadership training and ecumenical work camps in post war torn Europe and Asia. In the 1960s there was a radical change in the attitudes and activities of youth and students. It was the period of decolonization in Africa and the Caribbean and the Pacific. In Latin America and in Asia Christian youth and students were in the vanguard of resistance against undemocratic regimes. In the USA they were involved in the civil rights movement, and later were protesting against the Vietnam war. Everywhere students were raising questions about the undemocratic structures of the university, and the lack of a community of professors and students – *universitas magistrorum et scholarium* and *civitas academica* as it was expressed in the Middle Ages. They were calling for radical university reform, as well as for a more just and peaceful society. In May 1968, students in Paris rallied together under the slogan: 'Be realist, attempt the impossible.' This led to the further radicalization of youth and students, which had consequences for church youth and student work and for the Student Christian Movements. The sad story from the 1970s is that youth and students have been largely on the edges of the life of the churches and of the universities. The small efforts at university reform have been definitely reduced. Students are hardly active in the life of the university or of the SCM. Does this fact deeply concern the churches and the university professors? Are we satisfied especially with the quality of life and relationships in the universities today? This is a matter hardly discussed as a theological issue by groups like ourselves gathered in this symposium. Why is this so and what is to be done about it, especially by professors, not least in the theological faculties?

Mission and Evangelism. I was secretary for mission, international affairs, foreign students and world student relief in the British SCM in 1948 to 1950. In 1961 to 1966 I was secretary for West Africa and West Indies for the Methodist Missionary Society in Britain. Then followed six years as director of the Commission on World Mission and Evangelism of the WCC.

In the 1960s there was a vigorous study on 'The Missionary Structure of the Congregation' in Europe and North America, and also a series of in-depth surveys on 'Churches in Mission on Six Continents'. One result was a study report entitled, in the words of Dietrich Bonhoeffer, 'The Church for Others'. There was hope that these studies and surveys would stimulate, for example, the Volkskirche in Germany to undertake a radical enquiry on and overhaul of the established structures of the church, with its Constantinian heritage, in order to undertake more effectively the task of mission in Germany and in the rest of the world. All that basically happened was adding more instruments for attempting to meet the needs of various forms of mission and service, but not in the spirit of the Uppsala Assembly statement in 1968 on 'Renewal in Mission', which envisaged mutual thought and action both in North and South. Recent events, like the hasty merger of the church in the former DDR with the EKD, and the hesitant attitudes of the church hierarchies and bureaucracies to any consideration of reform for the sake of a relevant witness to an increasingly indifferent population, point to the fact that we have an urgent question before us of the future of the church in Germany. This can also be said about churches in many countries, with their own peculiar structural and cultural heritages. Jürgen Moltmann has given considerable attention to these concerns in his major writings. I hope that he will continue to wrestle with the necessary form and structure of the church as a whole as he so helpfully does about the congregations.

In the 1960s we developed a special unit within the WCC on Dialogue with People of Living Faiths and Ideologies. In the period after Vatican II, there was active co-operation with the Vatican bodies and the religious orders on this vital issue and on other matters related to Common Witness. This led to great debates within the fellowship of the WCC, and especially at the Fifth Assembly at Nairobi in 1975, following the conference of the Commission on World Mission and Evangelism in Bangkok in 1973. At the Assembly at Vancouver in 1983 it was possible to say:

Dialogue may be described as that encounter where people holding different claims about ultimate reality can meet and explore these claims in a context of mutual respect. From dialogue we expect to discern more about how God is active in our world, and to appreciate for their own sake the insights and experiences people of other faiths have of ultimate reality.

Since then these dialogues have continued. Christians and persons of other faiths have cooperated in working for

70

human rights and dignity, and for justice and peace. But in recent years, there has been growing fanaticism in various faiths, including among Christians. The question is how the dialogue so effectively undertaken over the years can become a means of exercising a ministry of reconciliation in different parts of the world. Given the present tendency to extremes and to destabilizing peoples and nations, this is a priority concern for all of us and not least university theological professors. Professor Hans Küng is making an important contribution to this ongoing dialogue.

World Council of Churches. My direct responsibility for the affairs of the whole WCC was from 1972 to 1984. These years were very controversial, especially in relation to the East–West and North–South conflicts, which were reflected in the relations between the churches and with the WCC. Some of the authorized programmes of the Council, like the Programme to Combat Racism, posed very direct questions to the attitudes and actions of the churches.

At the Nairobi Assembly in 1975 I said that the Assembly would 'have failed in its purpose if we did not advance to a new covenant relationship between churches at all levels of their life and the world at all levels of its activities'. At the Vancouver Assembly in 1983 I had to ask: 'Can the churches go on behaving as though the Council belongs to their external rather than their internal relations? . . . Can the churches conduct themselves as though they exist in isolation from each other and from their fellowship in the World Council, carrying on their programmes and activities with little relation with other churches around the world?' These questions and appeal were related to an earlier discussion in 1950 concerning 'the ecclesiological significance of the World Council of Churches'. So far as I can observe, there is little difference since 1983 in the relations between the member churches, including the Evangelical Church in Germany, and the World Council. As we are coming to the fiftieth anniversary of the Council in 1998, these issues will have to be faced. In essence the whole matter is a theological one and concerns the future not only of the World Council, but of the member churches. What contribution are theologians prepared to bring to this crucial ecclesiological debate?

In the 1970s the WCC was challenged to promote the community of women and men in church and society. In 1974 there was a very lively and productive conference in Berlin on the theme 'Sexism in the 1970s'. At the Nairobi Assembly in 1975 it was agreed to carry out a programme of study and action. By 1981 there was a world conference at Sheffield, England, when Elisabeth Moltmann-Wendel and Jürgen Moltmann conducted an excitingly effective dialogue on 'Becoming Human in New Community'. The WCC had to look at its own structures of representation on committees and staff. Of particular importance was to secure that at least 30% of the delegates at the Vancouver Assembly in 1983 would be women. This percentage has since gone up. Several churches have been guided to ordain women into the ministry and to elect women to the highest offices in their structures. In 1988 an International Decade of Churches in Solidarity with Women was launched.

Reference must also be made to the work which the Council, even before it was officially founded in 1948, had done in contributing to the drafting of the Universal Declaration of Human Rights which was adopted by the United Nations in December 1948. The Commission of the Churches on International Affairs also contributed to the work on the Covenants on Individual and Political Rights and on Social and Economic Rights. At a consultation in 1974 an important statement on 'Human Rights and Christian Responsibility' was produced. This was a contribution to the 1975 Helsinki Conference on Security and Cooperation in Europe. We all greatly profited from the splendid work and writings which Jürgen Moltmann has been doing on human rights – which has had a wide influence on the churches' theological thinking and witness. Related to this has been the work of the Council through the CCIA on disarmament and peace. However, considerable impetus was given to this concern by the massive march during the 1981 Kirchentag in Hamburg and in succeding years by committed groups of Christians in Germany. The WCC Public Hearing on Nuclear Weapons and Disarmament in Amsterdam in November 1981 had a formidable array of nuclear scientists and military strategists, not least from the USSR and the USA, as well as theologians and disarmament activists and politicians. This meeting and its follow-up posed questions to the churches, including the following: 'Can the churches agree on the theological and ethical basis for their stand on nuclear weapons and nuclear war? . . . Can the churches agree on effective political action to stop the production of, reduce and eventually abolish nuclear weapons? . . . How are the churches to relate to the new peace movements which are campaigning against nuclear arms?' The report of that public hearing carried the ominous title: 'Before it is too late'.

Globalization of Capitalist Economics and Finance. The concern for economic and social justice has been on the ecumenical agenda since the Stockholm Conference on Life and Work in 1925. Already in 1937 the Oxford Conference on Church, Community and State drew attention to the fact that 'centres of economic power have been formed which are not responsible to any organ of the community and which in practice constitute something in the nature of a tyranny over the lives of the masses of people'. At the first Assembly of the World Council of Churches in 1945 this devastating insight was softened by the statement: 'A responsible society is one where freedom is the freedom of persons who acknowledge responsibility to justice and public order and where those who hold political authority or economic power are responsible for its exercise to God and the people whose welfare is affected by it.'

After the Second World War there was certainly an effort on the part of Western powers to find ways to control economic power so that wealth may be more fairly distributed. This was in response in part to the challenge of the Soviet Union, where the economy and finance were completely under state control, but where people were denied political freedom. In the next twenty years the Western states went through a process of decolonization and of offering development aid. But this was on the terms laid down by these powerful nations, in connivance with corrupt and authoritarian rulers in the Third World. Moreover, a new phenomenon of uncontrolled centres of power came into being – the transnational corporations.

However, the WCC World Conference on Church and Society in 1966 saw hope in the new science-based technologies contributing to the development of the two-thirds poor world through international agencies. And so did the 1968 Uppsala Assembly. One of these agencies was the UN Commission on Trade and Development (UNCTAD), whose task was to negotiate a just price for eighteen key primary products of Third World countries. The WCC supported these moves and by 1970 set up its own commission on the Churches' Participation in Development. By 1974 a special session of the UN General Assembly produced a statement on 'Towards a New World Economic Order'. What seemed to encourage this ideal was the oil money being lavishly loaned by banks and governments to poorer countries. But UNCTAD was not able to persuade the rich countries to pay a just price for Third World products. Nevertheless, the WCC continued to call on the affluent states to make available a modest percentage of their assets to the Third World. In 1975, the WCC agreed to have as a guideline the

74

promotion of 'a just participatory and sustainable society', and in 1983 the Vancouver Assembly took up the challenge 'to engage the member churches in a conciliar process of mutual commitment (covenant) to justice, peace and the integrity of creation'.

It was only after the Assembly that some of us became suddenly aware of the fact that we had failed to raise the alarm after what had happened to Mexico in October 1982 when it defaulted in paying the massive interest on foreign loans. It was then that the two watch-dogs of the powerful Western nations, set up in 1944 as the International Monetary Fund and the World Bank, came into the picture and imposed structural adjustments, which have since been ruthlessly applied to the Third World debtor countries. These adjustments demanded substantial cuts in government spending on health, education and other social services, privatization of public utilities, and concentration on certain export crops or products. This has been disastrous, as I myself witnessed at close quarters in Jamaica during my stay there in 1985–1990. Another fact which became operative was that the more or less fixed rate of interest on the loans became higher and higher, after the US dollar was withdrawn from the gold standard in 1971. One clear example of the effect of floating of the dollar, generally upwards, is that the countries of Africa have for the last few years been subsidizing the creditor nations by over US $2 billion annually, in spite of the fact that the increased interest paid has already covered the original loans.

Perhaps the most decisive event was the break-up of the Soviet empire, and the consequent global supremacy of Western capitalism, armed with the panoply of vastly sophisticated science-based technology, government deregulation of the economy and finance, and privatization of various public services. During the past few years, these realities in the industrialized world have accelerated com-

75

petitiveness of a kind which forces mergers of various enterprises or 'slimming' in order to consolidate resources and be much less labour-intensive. Governments are also cutting back on health, education and social services. All this has brought about sharp unemployment or underemployment in industrialized countries and much unrest among the people.

A more staggering fact is that, with the rapid development of computers and of the means of communication, the movement of capital and what is called 'casino finance' has become even more dominant than ever. It is reckoned that in every twenty-four hours more than US $1,500 billion are circulating freely around the globe. Moreover, there are finance havens in different parts of the world which 'launder' money and provide the possibilities for huge fortunes to escape taxation by their countries of origin.

Furthermore, the globalized, competitive economic system is now monitored by a special institute in Lausanne, Switzerland. The institute also organises every year a meeting in Davos, where what are called 'global leaders' gather together in large numbers. At the conference in February this year some astonishing pronouncements were made. For example, the head of the great Swiss transnational corporation Nestlé said: 'Whether one is an individual, a major industry or a country, what is important for survival in this world is to be more competitive than the other.' Then Hans Tietmeyer, president of the Deutsche Bundesbank, also said that if the political authorities did not support this competitive line, 'the markets would sanction the government immediately, because the politicians are from now on under the control of the financial markets'. This last statement was clearly indicating that in this globalized economic and financial system, governments have little real power as the elected representatives of even a wealthy nation like Germany. They are in danger of being perceived to be the servants of the financiers and not of the people. This trend is worldwide and will become more obviously so before the end of this century. But I wonder whether we are not heading for a major crisis, more devastating than that of 1929.

In this new situation, the question must be posed as to whether we can do theology without taking seriously into account this frighteningly all-embracing competitive economic and financial system. This applies in particular to those few theologians, like Jürgen Moltmann, Johann Baptist Metz and Dorothee Sölle, who have so helpfully been articulating a political theology. Certainly we shall all have to embark on an urgent interdisciplinary study and research with colleagues in the universities, institutes, and with concerned and informed Christian groups who are seeking to grapple with the complex issues of the economy and finance.

In the earlier years of the World Council of Churches many people found it difficult to pronounce the word 'ecumenical' (concerning the whole inhabited earth). They would often say 'economical'! Nowadays, the pundits of the prevailing global finance and economic system freely use the word 'ecumenical' to give a certain religious solemnity to their almost godlike power. This, is, of course, in direct contradiction to the biblical use of the word *oikoumene*. For instance, the Psalmist sings: 'The earth is the Lord's, and the fullness of it, the world (*oikoumene*) and those who dwell in it' (24.1). And in the book of Isaiah, there is a song in which the prophet addresses God: 'When your judgments are in the earth, the inhabitants of the world *(oikoumene)* learn righteousness' (26.9). And righteousness, justice, in Hebrew *sedeq,* means right relations with God, with one's self and with others, and also with creation.

The present global, free economic and financial market operates in ways which benefit only a minority of the world's population. In many parts of the globe whole peoples are excluded from the system and from any viable existence. And yet, as the Epistle to the Ephesians reminds us, God's plan,

77

economy *(oikonomia),* declares the promise of inclusion when it indicates that it is 'for the fullness of time, to unite all things in Christ, things in heaven and things on earth' (1.9–10). Furthermore, in his letter to the dispersed churches in Asia Minor, the apostle Peter exhorts Christians: 'As each has received a gift, employ it for one another, as good stewards *(oikonomoi,* economists) of the varied grace of God' (I Peter 4.10). Indeed, in God's purpose the economy is for the well-being of all and the inclusion of all in God's grace, God's self-giving love. It is in this spirit that we must challenge and expose the present idolatrous global economic and financial system.

Hans Küng

What is there still to say? Everything dealt with, everything to some extent answered. It is not easy to be the last in what seems to me to have been a glorious series of fascinating statements. Having myself also lived through all those long years, I too could have said something similar about everything. But I have kept quiet, and after lunch, as after a Roman siesta, I have ordered my thoughts yet again. So I shall now similarly attempt to say in twenty minutes what seems important to me, nor in a preformulated way, but frankly and spontaneously.

'He really hasn't changed!' I have always regarded it as a great compliment on returning to my small country town of Sursee by Lake Lucerne when my schoolfriends have remarked, 'He really hasn't changed.'

So is it *semper idem*, 'always the same'? That really isn't my motto, but rather the motto of one of my first great opponents, one of the three Grand Inquisitors with whom I was confronted in a very personal and very threatening way. *'Semper idem'* was the saying that Cardinal Alfredo Ottaviani bore on his coat of arms. He was a very impressive type, and already half-blind when I made his acquaintance. Whatever one thought of him, one would certainly not have disputed that he had always remained the same. But immutability, this reflection of the *immutabilitas Dei*, this 'unchangeability of God' which I investigated critically almost at the same time as Jürgen Moltmann, in connection with Hegel and christology, was not of course my ideal.

Yet – and I also heard this in Jörg Zink's contribution – identity is a presupposition. And if today I were no longer identical with myself, I could no longer stand by the life that I have lived. So identity, but not conformity, is my first answer to the question that I have been asked. I have never kept riding the last wave in theology, nor have I thought much of others who have done so.

But of course one was thrown into quite specific constellations. I have kept asking myself: what distinguishes me, since we are all Catholics, from someone like Cardinal Ottaviani or later Cardinal Seper, or finally Cardinal Ratzinger? After all, we are all in the same church, believe in the same God, the same Jesus Christ, the same Spirit – and yet are quite different and believe differently. Perhaps that will also help you to understand why the concept of paradigm, the overall constellation, later made it possible for me to rationalize this basic difference in all the identity. These brothers in faith lived spiritually in another world, age, world-age, in another constellation, in another paradigm.

Now this paradigm – and here I am leaving aside everything personal and all church history – was the same one in which I had grown up. Indeed, remarkably, I am an archetypal insider where what I now call the Roman Catholic paradigm, the mediaeval paradigm, is concerned. I know my Denzinger, I know my Thomas Aquinas. No one can approach me with some interpretation of some dogma which I cannot so to speak test against the sources as it were off the cuff. We learned that for seven years, in Latin. We are firm in official doctrine. We also learned to think clearly. We could not carry on the kind of wishy-washy discussions that one can now carry on in German; certainly not in examinations where clear Latin terms, definitions and arguments were required.

So to the present day I am grateful for all that I received in Rome. No, I never had any 'anti-Roman feeling' such as Hans Urs von Balthasar used to like to foist on me. I could say a great deal about that, but now is not the time.

However, of course at a very early stage I noticed that some things just were not done. No, it wasn't all that early, but only after about five years. Still, I don't want to talk about that now. I must simply say that in the end I could not avoid putting the Roman system in question, particularly in theology, in vigorous arguments in the Collegium Germanicum, lasting for months, which affected my health. It became clear to me that this neoscholastic scheme could not be sustained. At that time the question of infallibility was not the central question, although of course already at that stage people were asking whether what a pope like Pius XII was promulgating almost every day was infallible or not; that was the time when the pope said that a mother had to give up her life if the life of her child could be saved, and so on. What the Pope said at that time was regarded as in fact infallible; at any rate, no one dared to contradict it in public. If one did that, things became dangerous. So to this degree this question of ultimate authority came to a head at a very early stage.

Be this as it may, I know the doctrine of infallibility so thoroughly that no one can fool me over it. And no one in Rome has ever claimed that I have exaggerated on matters of infallibility. That has been claimed only in Germany, by all those Catholic theologians who wanted to avoid this question because it was too dangerous. They said that I was exaggerating; but nothing was exaggerated, as was proved time and again. For what the Congregation of Faith has recently promulgated in the Pope's name about the impossibility of the ordination of women, which is an infallible doctrine, is quite clearly a consequence of the thesis that I learned at the Gregorian and that now unfortunately appears in article 25 of the Vatican II Constitution on the Church about the *magisterium ordinarium,* i.e. that quite everyday teaching office of the Pope and the bishops, which is said to be just as infallible as the *magisterium extraordinarium* of a papal *ex cathedra* statement or the definition of a council. It became clear to me as early as the 1960s that that wasn't on.

Karl Rahner – this is now a further stage – and with him also the French, above all Henri de Lubac and Yves Congar, whom I got to know personally at a very early stage (but let's leave out the biography), was a very great stimulus. Rahner flung open all the doors in the great building of neo-scholasticism. He stormed into every room, turned everything around and reorganized it, and then went straight on into another room, where once again he moved everything around and thought that he had now settled the problems. However, in time I saw through Rahner's thought as a verbal dialectic which in practice made it possible for him to say: ' "Outside the church no salvation." But, if one shakes around all these terms, "outside", "no", "church" "salvation", one can also say the opposite, "Also outside the church salvation, indeed outside the church much salvation." ' After all, everyone is an 'anonymous Christian'. However, he didn't venture to say that all these should even be 'anonymous Catholics'. In short, for Rahner that wasn't on.

Subsequently I felt it a tragic development for Catholic theology that Rahner and I should have fallen out on the publication of my book in 1970. But the book had to be written, and if I had to write a book again, it would certainly be *Infallible? An Enquiry*. It had to be written, and there has still been no response to its enquiry. Even in Tübingen people do not dare to give a clear answer to this question, because everyone knows what then happens from the church authorities, namely what happened to me. That, briefly, on the first paradigm, the Roman Catholic paradigm which has come to us from the Middle Ages, reinforced by the Counter-Reformation, and given an anti-modernist focus by neoscholasticism. It is a constellation which I had to give up, since it was inappropriate both to our time and to the gospel.

I regarded it as a great gain that already in Rome I came across the theology of the Protestant theologian Karl Barth. Indeed I not only came across it, but studied it so thoroughly – for my theological licentiate at the Gregorian in Rome and my doctorate in Paris – that since then I have known Barthian theology as thoroughly as neoscholasticism. This has also made it possible for me to understand the Protestant theologians – down to their ultimate intentions. One mustn't just see the great architecture of Barth's *Dogmatics,* which I too admire, as I admire that of Schleiermacher. In addition, the fact that in our century, too, a theologian appeared who said what mattered, what the Christian cause is, and that we cannot dissolve God's word and revelation into psychology and the history of religion, that gave me firm ground under my feet – and still does.

In a phase during which I had to work out for myself how to get through a critical period, it seemed to me tremendous that I could study such great theology in Rome, in Switzerland and in Paris. And also being able to get to know Karl Barth very well personally (but these again are personal matters which do not belong here) has shaped my whole life. Moreover I must say that the justification of the sinner in Barthian and Catholic theology, which was the topic of my dissertation, has remained theologically and spiritually central for me down to the present day. Justification of the sinner – that is my existence: that one is not justified by works, even by one's theological works, but by faith, by unshakeable trust in God himself. That is basic for a Christian, and I have always held firm to it, particularly when it became difficult. *Sola fide* – understood in a good Catholic way, as I demonstrated in my 1957 book. And I can only laugh at all those Catholic and Protestant theologians who still keep forming commissions and having endless discussions about justification, justification, justification. That is no longer the problem; even Ratzinger agrees with me on that. But of course the consequences of the message of justification, say, for church order, for ministry, for the papacy, but in another way, also for the meaning of life, is another question. In short, in this way I not only got to know the Reformation, the Reformation paradigm, at an early stage but could also integrate it into my theology. So I no longer have any difficulties when I look back on the controversies of the sixteenth century. Protestant concentration with Catholic breadth: since then that has continued to be my slogan.

Yes, we are no longer in the sixteenth century. And I now have to say – and this distinguishes me from some of my Protestant colleagues in Tübingen – that at the latest when I came to Tübingen I discovered that I had to take historical criticism (a result of the paradigm of modernity) no less seriously than Barthian theology. I have been somewhat shaken that no one in this colloquium has spoken of historical criticism. As far as I can remember, there has not even been a mention of it in all these statements.

But, I want to ask, can one do without it? Yes, of course I already know what my dear friends here will all say: that they already have all these theological things behind them, that they go back to Bultmann, and so on. Yes, one can go back to Bultmann, and for example leave out all his demythologizing and simply practise existential interpretation. But if one keeps bracketing off these points, which have been disputed since the Enlightenment, it isn't surprising that not-so-new books like those of Lüdemann in Protestant theology should have caused such a tremendous stir. Why? Because these questions aren't being dealt with clearly either in lectures or in books. One has only to start asking questions: 'What is your view of death and the devil, hell and original sin? What is the exegetical basis of christology? Do you believe that you can justify your doctrine of the Trinity on a historical-critical basis?' [Intervention by Jüngel, 'Yes!'

Laughter.] Then, yes then, one gets apodictic answers like that *[laughter]*, but the basis for them is not given anywhere as a theological issue *[laughter]*. Yes, now you can see how things are getting lively.

In short, I am eternally grateful that a Tübingen scholar who is not here, but from whom we have all learned, Ernst Käsemann, has developed the work of Bultmann, his teacher, has understood it and at the same time criticized it and corrected it in quite decisive points: not just historicity but real history; not just futurity, but the real future; not just worldliness, being in the world, but the real world and society as it exists today; not just the Christ of the kerygma but the Jesus of history. For me this Jesus of history, the Crucified and Risen One, has become central. Without Käsemann I doubt whether I would have had the courage to write my book *On Being a Christian* from the perspective of the Jesus of history, from below. For me this Jesus of history, who cannot be separated from the Christ of proclamation, remains the concrete centre of theology. This is the theological basis of my identity. But I can understand this centre, after the Enlightenment, only in the light of historical criticism. And my diagnosis at this point is that the reason for the wretched state of theology today, both Protestant and Catholic, lies precisely here: in the hiatus, in the monstrous gulf between the results of historical criticism and learned dogmatics. I know that there are dogmatic theologians today who think that they have overcome this hiatus, but I have never really seen how. And I remember a conversation with Eberhard Jüngel in which he himself put the question, 'Have we really done it?' I quietly thought that I had done it for myself.

So to be brief, for me that has remained. The centre of my theology has remained constant, but the horizon has constantly changed. And I fully agree with Philip Potter: the Bible and the newspaper. The Bible, the gospel; yes, for me the centre is not even simply 'the gospel', but this Jesus Christ himself, as a person, with all that he has to say, what he fought for and suffered. He, the Crucified and Risen Lord, is and remains the centre. But at the same time there is the constantly changing horizon, the newspaper. Everything that has been given one by time, what moves, has motivated one.

Once it had become clear to me where I stand, what is the centre and what the horizon, I attempted to go further in a consistent way. I have not made any great zig-zags in my theological career; here perhaps I differ from my friend and colleague Jürgen Moltmann. He went from the theology of the resurrection to the theology of the cross and then again from the theology of revolution to the theology of play. Here I am rather more boring, rather less antithetical, or if you like, simply 'catholic' – in the best sense. You are right to laugh: the Catholic way consists less in demarcations than in comprehensive integration – though for me that is becoming constantly more critical. Despite my militant image, throughout my theology I am always concerned more with integration than demarcation, and here with constantly learning, assimilating new things, setting out for new shores.

Indeed, once the stone, my decision to engage in academic theology (rather than practical pastoral care), had been thrown into the water, the course of my thought could be compared with concentric circles extending further and further, though this was not planned in any way, but provoked by the challenges of the time. Concentric circles: thus in the 1950s with the topic of justification my concern was with the theological foundation of Christian existence. In the 1960s I concentrated on the questions of council, church and reunion, culminating in the books on the church and the question of infallibility. In the 1970s my research was into the foundations of theology and christology, initiated by my book on Hegel's christology and followed by *On Being a Christian, Does God Exist?* and *Eternal Life.* In the 1980s, after the great conflict with Rome in December 1979, came my now intensive preoccupation with the world religions, but also with questions of hermeneutics, the paradigm shift, ecumenical theology *ad extra*. Finally in the 1990s, I turned to the religious situation of humankind generally: alongside works on world literature, music and psychotherapy above all the global ethic project, with historical and systematic analyses of Judaism, Christianity and – hopefully – Islam, all of which has finally been given continuity by the Global Ethic Foundation. All this has certainly been slow work, but work with great intensity, and of course I could go on at great length about 'how my mind has changed'.

The term 'global ethic' finally expresses everything which in the post-modern paradigm is unconditionally necessary for the survival of humankind as a basic consensus of binding values, irrevocable norms and urgently necessary attitudes. To work this out and carry it through is a giant task, and I am delighted that now more and more young theologians, Catholic and Protestant, are joining in this great project. But here and now my time is up. At any rate, I still enjoy life and doing theology, and I hope that I shall long continue to do so.

Television Discussion

Presenter: Hans Norbert Janowski

Janowski

They have made theological history and written many important books. They have taught in lecture rooms, discussed at church conferences and in the ecumenical movement, and taken part in the ecology movement and the peace movement. Above all they have left their stamp on generations of theology students with their thought and their commitment. A generation of Protestant and Catholic theologians have spent the whole of today taking stock. Where have their different, often idiosyncratic ways really led? Of course questions have remained open and there are unresolved problems, quite apart from the new questions posed by the next generation. Obviously, one central question is: what will become of the message and fellowship of Christians if more and more people are turning away from the churches but at the same time the quest for meaning in life is becoming more intense, if church membership is declining but a religious sense is increasing?

Welcome to this discussion on the theological tasks of the future. We shall be carrying on the conversation in two rounds. First, what is to be done and what is not to be done? Does peace call for a shared ethic? What is the meaning of Christian discipleship in a pluralistic world of cultures, religions and fashions? Hans Küng, Dorothee Sölle, Elisabeth Moltmann-Wendel and Jörg Zink will discuss these political and ethical questions.

The second round, with Eberhard Jüngel and Johann

Baptist Metz, and then Jürgen Moltmann and Philip Potter, will try to discover the spirit and the fellowship in which Christians can live if traditional forms of life like the family and also the church community dissolve, and solidarity comes to be on short supply.

Until recently Hans Küng was Director of the Institute for Ecumenical Research in the University of Tübingen. He is well known not only as a result of his conflict with Rome but even more through his great books, not least the great little book *Global Responsibility*. Jörg Zink hardly lags behind him in the number of his publications. They offer guidance above all in questions of faith and life. Zink is a landmark of the German Evangelical Kirchentag, and is also well known for his Sunday broadcasts over many years. Professor Dorothee Sölle began her course into political theology with a chapter 'theology after the death of God'; she has been stimulated by Latin American liberation theology and has also left a lasting mark on the development of feminist theology. Elisabeth Moltmann-Wendel also plays an influential role in feminist theology in this country, and is active as a mediator between the fronts and as the mentor of many younger theologians.

Professor Küng, theology and the church often make statements, and about almost everything. And when they do, they usually say nothing different from other responsible bodies. Many people have stopped listening to them. Should they really restrict themselves, and if so, to what?

Küng
You've asked the most difficult question right at the start. First of all, I think that we must simply recognize that the churches are caught up in a structural crisis. This isn't an ordinary crisis; it has been coming upon us for a long time, and there are many ways in which we have failed to develop. Many of the things that we deal with in the churches are no

longer interesting. We still have a great commission working on questions relating to the sixteenth century. Nowadays reasonable theologians can basically sort out all the things that separated Catholics and Protestants at that time. We have failed to develop in other directions: I need only mention the question of the role of women, which will certainly come up again soon. Of course people are asking 'What must be done now?' You're quite right in saying that we cannot simply go on saying what everyone else is saying. Of course we must all recognize that. Time and again there are theologians, happily not those on the platform here, who talk about things which they really don't understand very well. And there are also church governments which give the impression of always lagging behind.

Let me mention just the most recent issue in which I've been involved, namely the question of euthanasia. Here we are being told the old story that it isn't a simple matter. As if we didn't all know that! Why must the Protestant church now parrot everything that the Roman church has already said on this subject? There is no disputing the fact that this is a very serious question. But here the churches really should be in the vanguard, spiritually in the vanguard, and not constantly in the rearguard. And if you also ask, 'All right, then what must remain?', I would go on to say, 'Yes, of course we must be central – whether the question is one of life and death, or of the role of women, or of church order. We must speak from our centre.' Of course if, as often happens in church declarations, what we have to say as Christians and in an enlightened Christianity isn't clear enough, then it cannot be convincing. This centre where we stand, which is our standpoint, must be clear, so that of course it has the greatest possible openness.

You can see that that isn't very easy by considering another question which will presumably be asked here – though I don't know what would happen if we began to argue here on the platform. Does faith in Jesus Christ also allow other men and women to be saved? At any rate, there are certainly theologians in Tübingen who think that such people cannot be saved. Only Christians can be saved, therefore there must be mission. My view is that while mission is possible, testimony is preferable to mission. But here one can see – and this is a concrete point – that at the same time it must be proved that for us (to put it quite plainly) this Christ remains the way, the truth and the life. Otherwise we wouldn't know what Christianity should really be. But at the same time we can combine that with the maximum degree of openness which – and here I am proud to have been at Vatican II – assures even atheists of good faith who are acting in accordance with their conscience that they can be saved. This is tremendous progress beyond what people used to say, 'Outside the church no salvation.' But that would be a task which, I believe Protestant theology hasn't yet solved, and the World Council of Churches hasn't yet solved. So it would be a quite central point.

Janowski
In the dialogue of the religions which is so overdue, thank God the question is not so much whether there is salvation outside Christianity but rather whether it is possible for the religions to arrive at a common ethic. You have said that there can be no peace in the world without peace between the religions. A look at the Balkans or the Middle East confirms that. So you have argued vigorously for such a dialogue of religions and for a shared global ethic. But isn't it quite impossible in the kind of multicultural world in which we live to establish an ethic, even if this only amounts to the recognition of human rights?

Küng
First of all I want to draw a distinction between human rights and ethics. Since the French Revolution we have had the

unresolved problem – and this was already stated in 1789 in the National Assembly in Paris in the middle of the Revolution – that if now we define only rights, then afterwards all will have rights. But what about responsibilities? Everyone will fall out over their rights, and that is what we have today. All have rights, and the rights are always rights over against others. In the end ethics also includes responsibilities, and consciousness of this has, I have to say, kept increasing. I could now cite two or three UN commissions from the last two or three years where a global ethic comes at the beginning, in a very long chapter. Why? Because meanwhile people have come to see that the religions do not just comprise fanatics who attack others violently. It has been noted in UNESCO and in other bodies that there are also people who can help to introduce peace. And the decisive point is this. Though there may be disagreements among Christians, Jews and Muslims – and probably many other religions too – over many questions of faith, and it is inconceivable that there could be a shared religion in the foreseeable future (nor is that to be aimed at), there must be peace between the religions. The decisive point is that if one looks at the great traditions, from the Decalogue in the Hebrew Bible to – shall we say – the Buddhist canon, the great discourses are the same when it comes to ethics. And it would once again be infinitely worthwhile if people were now aware of that again in concrete terms. What does it really mean today, for children, too, who see only violence on the television (and we live in a time when there are an increasing number of child murders and teenage murders), that once it was said 'You shall not kill'? Of course this has to be said time and again. I might add that at any rate in 1993, the Parliament of the World's Religions in Chicago passed a whole Declaration Toward a Global Ethic which describes all these things in a very concrete way and shows that here a consensus is possible, though of course it is a minimal consensus. But a very great deal, an infinite amount, would have been achieved if people were once again aware of these minimal things.

Janowski
Jörg Zink, you have drawn quite a different conclusion with your commitment, which now goes back many years. You've taken a particular course in order to be credible as a theologian. Or perhaps you've even left some theology behind you. You joined a party, the 'Greens', at a time when some people still took offence at such a step. Shouldn't a theologian really keep out of party politics? Doesn't he endanger his ethical and social credibility, since his preaching is addressed to everyone?

Zink
I don't see why a theologian should keep out of politics. I am a citizen of this land. I share in the rights and responsibilities which all citizens of this land have. Among these rights is that of joining an assembly in which one thinks that one can achieve one's aims, even if that is a political party. If one joins a social organization, no one objects. If one joins a political party, things are always difficult. And in the decisive phases of political development over the last forty years our churches have constantly told their pastors, 'Please keep quiet; please say nothing; please hold back, you will offend someone.' I just don't see it. Already as a young man I watched what was happening to the landscape of my homeland, through the building of roads, through destruction and poison. After that I lived through a war in which we drove in our tanks straight across the fields almost to Moscow. And since then I have seen a whole society tearing apart the legacy that it owes to its children and grandchildren. I have seen how we always deal with what has to be deal with by leaving for our children the work and tasks and sacrifices that

we should be engaged in. That has been the principle by which our agricultural policy has been shaped. As early as 1965 I made a couple of films for television about the destruction of the environment, the creation. For me that was primarily a theological topic, and then also a political topic. Then I saw that not a single party in this country was tackling this problem seriously; they didn't even see it, let alone get down to it. And for me it was a great experience when in 1979 a whole lot of young people suddenly got together and said, 'We shall call ourselves "The Greens"; our symbol will be the sunflower and not the eagle, the bird of prey. We want to ensure that some air and water and earth is left for our children and grandchildren.' I am almost a founder member. I joined the movement at that time, among other things because the whole of the adult world was telling the young people, as it still does, 'You are chaotic, you are destructive, you are destroying all the political structures that we created.' And I thought that there should also be a few old people to speak up for the young. That's what I did, much to the annoyance of my church authorities.

Janowski
Did you ever regret it? Today the Greens are part of the establishment.

Zink
Later I had difficulties in supporting the Greens. That was at the time when the remainder of the 1968 movement had seized control. Then much was distorted, and suddenly the environment was not so important as changing society. At that time there were many illusions, and that had not originally been the case in ecological politics. Then I hardly took any part in it and simply gave a bit of advice now and again. I've also sometimes wondered whether I should get out of the wretched business, but I remained in it, because

I didn't expect to get out. Now I can see how this movement is beginning again, how it is becoming real and practical and responsible, and so far I have had no reason to look in another party for what I sought, namely a serious peace policy and a serious environmental policy. Of course originally I was a Social Democrat, but where could I find all that in the Social Democratic Party today? Someone ought to tell me some time. But as I've remarked, everyone else has the right to be involved in other political parties, and I hope that many pastors are. For if we have something to say, we should say it loudly. Why do we claim, as is asserted a million times, that a pastor should keep his mouth shut if he understands nothing about politics? We're a democracy. And in a democracy the basic assumption is that every citizen understands something of politics: the experts don't have the sole right to politics at the expense of everyone else. I'm an inhabitant of this land and a citizen, and therefore I have to have my say in politics.

Janowski
Now we go back a bit. Dorothee Sölle, your generation entered theology under the impact of a profound experience of death, war, annihilation, the Holocaust, genocide. Why, I sometimes wonder, didn't this experience take you away from God?

Sölle
An Israeli woman writer recently asked me precisely the same question. She said that most people in Israel are no longer believers for precisely that reason, whereas I claimed that that was why I became a Christian. I think that we have to ask ourselves what the alternatives were in this situation. What else could I have become? What options does one really have? For me the real alternative was nihilism, which I experienced and sensed from Albert Camus: a theoretic, ethical nihilism

for which I had great respect. Nevertheless, that was too cold for me, too remote in its relationship to the ground of existence, too abstract. I had something in my mind, a dimension; I had intimations of something more which has not yet been put into words, namely what it really means to love God with all one's heart, with all one's being, above all things. What it really means for there to be something like an *amour fou*, an absolute, crazy love, a love which really doesn't contribute anything, whether money or possessions or gifts, and doesn't even make one happy, as my friend Metz remarked earlier. It's a love of the ground of being, of this mystery of faith – or whatever one wants to call it – and words really play a subordinate role. But without this basic love neither ethics nor the church are worth anything, nor will they last, but rather perish. The Reformation always said that there is really no such thing as atheism. When people say that they do not believe in God, they believe in capitalism. This view that we are born to be capable of doing business is very widespread. That is the new ideal of *the homo oeconomicus*. People are there to do business, and to do it well.

I don't want to have anything to do with this kind of idolatry, which is absolutely the dominant idolatry for us. I want to live differently. And I believe that many people have a longing to live in quite a different way. That doesn't begin with a change of eating habits or other ethical questions in the narrower or wider sense, but at the spiritual level which I call mysticism. Without it nothing will change for us, not even our lifestyle. We will keep on destroying this earth as long as there is not this spirituality, of which Jörg Zink has spoken, and no one loves the creation so much as the mystery of life does.

Janowski
Can you say a few words about the direction of this mystical assurance, its connection with what you sometimes call the

politicizing of the conscience in resistance? That's the way you've taken. Can it really be handed on to others? Isn't the situation quite different, as you yourself also describe it after grappling with economics and capitalism in a world which has become very one-sided?

Sölle

I find my view confirmed. If this world is to survive, if our children or grandchildren are still to have water to drink, then we need different basic conditions and must continue to work on them. What is theology about if this *theos* is not concerned with that? If we don't pester this mystery of life, this deity, with our wishes, hopes and complaints; if we don't find another language for doing that? And I simply don't believe that one can dispense with something like religion. Now if that is taken seriously, it leads to what I shall describe with a great word, 'resistance'. It led to Sophie Scholl and Dietrich Bonhoeffer and to Oscar Arnulfo Romero and Martin Luther King and many, many others, to the point where they said 'no' to this world as it now is, to its barbarism. And they said it as clearly as they could with their life, their suffering, their habits, their taxes. Here was a passion for the absolute. That's the real issue, and it doesn't lead to a distracted inwardness, which I regard as pseudo-mysticism. Here I would want to dissociate myself from a will which closes its eyes and concentrates totally on the ego. I mean the tiresome neighbour, the ugly neighbour next door, who belongs in the heart of the deity, at any rate in our tradition.

Janowski

Elisabeth Moltmann, you've really looked at the things that Dorothee Sölle is now describing in a similar way, yet somewhat differently. You're pleading for a kind of new thinking, a new rationality as you call it, one which ought to mean that the command to love one's neighbour as oneself first of all involves self-respect and self-love. Only then has the presupposition for respect for the stranger been created. Do you think that a fixation on the sinner who needs grace and forgiveness is somewhat paralysing? Is that really still a biblical perspective on life?

Moltmann-Wendel
O yes, I think that that is precisely the biblical perspective, for this theology of the sinner which has developed in the course of church history has been used, for example, by the authorities in the dreadful dogma of original sin to keep people helpless and dependent. Elaine Pagels has described this very well. There are political connections between a theology of the sinner and political power. I would simply like to put a wedge between them and say that we should begin where Jesus really began. He came to make this creation whole again. He healed, made people whole again, he set them upright, and like Matthew Fox, of whom Jörg Zink also spoke, began with the original blessing of creation and not with original sin. That seems to me to be tremendously important, not as some discovery of new theology but as what we need in order to fulfil the many tasks that we have heard about here. Otherwise we cannot fulfil them. If I don't have the feeling of being good, whole and beautiful, as I have often said, and if I cannot deal with things with a good conscience, then I cannot do anything. I would like to mention something else which is important to me. The totality of a person, head and body, belongs together, including the feet, the hands, the senses, which are completely forgotten. They are only addressed to some degree by Catholics, but not by Protestants, and usually only in the wrong way. For me something begins here that I would describe as 'pleasure'. When I'm with Catholics and happen to mention the world 'pleasure' I notice a kind of quiver, like

an anxiety about pleasure, since it is tied up with sin. First of all we must rediscover these things which are shut up so deeply in our soul because they are forbidden, and find the way back to this pleasure and passion. Here I would like to add to what Dorothee Sölle has said that for me pleasure is also part of passion. No passion can arise without pleasure. But these are forbidden areas which are often connected with a misunderstanding of sexuality. However, for me they are deeply present in the gospel and also in the Old Testament. 'Delight in the Lord,' what does that mean?

Metz
If I might say something about the Catholic sense of life, if that's allowed, Elisabeth . . .

Moltmann-Wendel
Of course it is.

Metz
Recently I was asked in a similar broadcast, 'You're a sensible person, why are you a Catholic?' 'Precisely for that reason,' I replied in equally impudent terms and also mentioned some other trivial reasons for the difference between confessions: because I don't have to be as German as the Protestants, and then because as a Catholic I know rather more about the Jewish element in Christianity. And above all, and that's the only reason why I mention it here, 'I need have no inhibitions about eating and drinking.' So, Elisabeth, your mention of a quiver just isn't right. And of course love goes along with eating and drinking and cooking. Those are things which belong together.

Janowski
We're making a jump here. You've often written and said that not only pleasure, in eating or drinking and cooking, but

99

also suffering – and of course the sight of the suffering of Christ – can lead to a liberating experience, have a liberating power. The memory of suffering, you sometimes say, and thus also the churches' memory of what has been suffered, can be the impulse towards a change in conditions. How do you make that plausible?

Metz
Let me put it like this. In his parables Jesus spoke as it were to the heart of the world – for believers and unbelievers. The stories which to some degree have become background stories for our whole culture certainly include a parable like that of the good Samaritan, the story of his eyes, of attentiveness to the suffering of others, the readiness to listen more to the authority of a sufferer than to the call to the temple. Here I'm thinking of the priest and the levite who 'out of a higher interest' pass by the one who has fallen among robbers. This is the story of a mysticism which one can learn from Jesus: I've often called it a mysticism not of closed eyes but of open eyes, capable of perceiving the suffering of others, and if we're already speaking of the memory that has been preserved in the church, then this memory must beyond question always be an essential part of the memory of suffering, quite unsentimental, focussed on the suffering of others. It really goes without saying that the one who hears the resurrection of Christ in such a way as to forget the cry of his passion has not heard the gospel, but a kind of victory myth.

So I now think that the Christian memory of suffering – above all as the memory of the suffering of others – in fact has something to do with our present-day political life. Only this morning I referred to something that I would very much like to refer to here. Memories of suffering, memories of suffering relating to oneself which always remember only one's own history of suffering, are dangerous. Politically they have a destructive effect, and of course they know nothing of the messianic command to love one's enemy. In Yugoslavia all the ethnic groups have always referred only to their own history of suffering and sometimes played this off against other ethnic groups. That had to end in catastrophe. Of course that continues to be a critical question to the religious, Christian institutions there. But there are also examples to the contrary in the present-day political world: you may remember the first handshake between Arafat and Rabin, when each assured the other that they would now attempt to shape a policy of peace, in which they didn't think only of their own suffering, but refused to forget the suffering of the others, their former enemies, in their actions. Such an attitude has links with the biblical tradition.

I think that this is very important in our present situation. Many people say that we've reached a stage of moral exhaustion in Europe. There is said to be no such thing as 'universal morality', as European morality was at one time, in which the political enlightenment and the Ten Commandments of Mount Sinai were linked. It is even denounced by critical intellectuals as a 'moral trap'.

To that as Christians we oppose a quite ambitious statement which might go like this. Really there is no suffering whatsoever in the world that does not concern us. Inevitably one gets castigated for saying such things. But if one looks closer and listens, then this statement is really the basic statement of all the great constitutional democracies, since it is really none other than the moral consequence of taking the principle of the equality of all men and women seriously. And unless we take it seriously, the multicultural landscape of Europe may one day be a burning and not a flourishing landscape. Or our Europe might not continue to be a peaceful landscape, but become a landscape with escalating civil wars. So I ask you whether we do not have something here to contribute from our traditions which go back to the parable of Jesus with which I began.

And if I might say something quickly to Hans Küng. I think that this respect for the suffering of others can really also be a bridging category, a basic category in the encounter between religions and cultures. Perhaps it even has to be. I know no great culture and no great religion which is not stamped by this respect. And I know no claim to the truth to which I would bow that would not also always be ready to take note of the suffering of others in this truth and to express it.

Janowski
But isn't there also something left over here? One needn't just think of the murder of Rabin. How will you cope with the fact that suffering cannot be prevented, that murder goes on? These are old, famous questions which we cannot answer here, but perhaps you might reflect on them in this connection.

Metz
Here I can really only echo what Dorothee Sölle has already said. You know, if Christianity were only a morality and not a hope, if it were so to speak only a setting for ethics – and that's a great deal – and not for what the theologians call eschatology, then I really wouldn't know what to say which didn't drive me into scepticism and perhaps also into resignation.

Janowski
You will note that here we're talking in a language which isn't necessarily the language of theological tradition and the theological disciplines. That's no coincidence. On the other hand there is a theological language which has shaped and still shapes many people, with many words, some of which have become incomprehensible: grace, forgiveness, justification, sin. Professor Jüngel, can you help us out a bit here and loosen the tongue of this old theological language? What actually is sin?

Jüngel

Do you think that my speciality is the old and incomprehensible?

Janowski

No, but its redemption from the Babylonian captivity of language.

Jüngel

All right, I'll attempt to do that as the schoolmaster which I now am – schoolmaster is a fine professional designation for an ordinarius professor of theology.

What is sin? Sin is a theological expression for evil. But one can know evil only in terms of the good. Anyone who wants to say what is evil must know what is good. To put it pointedly in theological terms, one can only recognize sin in all its uncanny and evil nature where it is forgiven. That is very important for one's basic attitude to the whole phenomenon, since in that case the pointing finger of morality with which people want to tie others to the evil that they have done drops away quite automatically. To want to tie people to the evil that they have done is sanctimonious. And as theologians we have to train pastors and not sanctimonious clerics. So our whole concern with evil must centre on our attempting to define it in terms of the good, i.e. in terms of the gospel. Then one can first of all say, very roughly, that evil is everything that is aggressive against the good. Kierkegaard once said in a pointed way that sin is not granting oneself the good that God has intended. And I would add that sin is of course also not granting this good to others. But what is good? From the biblical texts one could perhaps say four things:

1. According to the biblical testimony, good is that on which one can rely unconditionally. And in Hebrew, that on which one can rely unconditionally is truth. The truth is what

is unconditionally reliable. That would mean that the primal form of evil, the primal form of sin, is the lie – not the intellectual lie, though that is also included, but the living lie which poisons and destroys everything and which has very urgently and very impressively been presented to us by Dorothee Sölle's contributions.

2. It is good to be, rather than not to be. In that case evil would be that aggression against being which says no to what God has created. And that already begins at the place where being as togetherness becomes a problem. Being is always being together.

3. Good is being in the form of being together successfully, not as the annexation of the other, nor as a uniformity which excludes the other. The Trinity which Küng does not rate very highly is a good example of the meaning of being as togetherness, namely a fellowship of mutual otherness. And human beings as the image of God should similarly be capable of a fellowship of mutual otherness. Evil is the destruction of this togetherness, this wealth of relationship. Evil is the pressure towards a lack of relationship, that lack of relationship which destroys togetherness.

4. Good is not only being created by God but also being willed and affirmed by God. To know that one is willed and affirmed is good. And correspondingly, it is evil to say no to that to which God has said yes. Some conclusions would need to be drawn from that for the meaning of the forgiveness of sins.

Janowski
Yes, in so far as forgiveness is really more than psychotherapy.

Jüngel
Psychotheraphy needs the doctor, forgiveness needs the almighty God. That is a considerable difference. Certainly

one can imagine God in the role of the doctor. That happens very impressively in Holy Scripture. But the forgiveness of sins is a legal act. This legal act says that your sinful past no longer concerns you; you are free of it. Being free from one's past is also an aspect of mysticism. You can allow yourself to see, and no one has the tight to tie you once again to this sinful past. But that also means that you yourself no longer have the right to tie yourself once again to this sinful past. However, the legal act is only the first thing. The second thing which must now follow immediately is this: the forgiveness of sins is an act of love. The wealth of relationships which have been destroyed by evil, by aggressiveness, by the removal of good, this wealth of relationships in life, is restored through the forgiveness of sins. Where all relations end and all conditions are destroyed, only love creates new relationships. Love is therefore really the only creative power. And in this sense the forgiveness of sins is the event of an act of love. Luther remarked that where there is forgiveness of sins, there is life and bliss. Life means being affirmed by God, and bliss means being whole, in peace with God and the whole of creation, and therefore also at peace with oneself: *shalom.*

Only forgiveness of sins makes possible that totality which you, dear Frau Moltmann, have rightly apostrophized. I understand what you're opposing. But I would want to point out that the danger of a misunderstanding is very great. I doubt whether one can banish sin from the world by keeping quiet about it.

Sölle
May I say something here?

Janowski
Yes, we're pressed for time, but do say it.

Sölle

What you've just said about evil reminded me of a great master of recent times. It was rather too pre-political and too friendly. The name of the master from whom I've learned a great deal is Bertholt Brecht, who said, 'Evil has an address, it has a telephone number.' I simply wanted to interject that in order to explain that we cannot simply dismiss what the Enlightenment says about evil. It doesn't just take place outside theology, so to speak quite elsewhere. We aren't just the ones who accuse ourselves. The naming of the names and addresses of evil is business, political business.

Jüngel

I thoroughly agree. That's why earlier today I called for the elaboration of a table of categories of evil which would achieve precisely that, as a task for the future. However, it has to be realized that evil goes round the best addresses. Isn't that so? It lives at the best addresses. It's not so simple to mention some of the addresses. Don't let's give any examples now.

Janowski

And also Frau Moltmann.

Moltmann-Wendel

We've just been given a very classical explanation of forgiveness, which for me derives from an authoritarian image of God. Here I would just like to interject that today this has become highly questionable for many people. It may still be taught in theological faculties, but in many spheres in which the church now takes place that is no longer the view, and that also has to be said.

Jüngel

Well, as long as I teach in theological faculties, the teaching will be of what is true, but not what you understand by that. It's hard to call God as the embodiment of love simply authoritarian. Is the one who creates new relationships where all relationships have been shattered authoritarian? No, that's a cliché, and we should get used to doing without clichés.

Moltmann-Wendel

Erich Fromm says that forgiveness and sin go together and derive from an authoritarian way of thinking. Healing and sickness go together, and that corresponds much more to modern men and women. And for me that is very Christian and Jewish. But we must see how forgiveness and sin go together and how they can also be expressed in a different way, which is not authoritarian.

Jüngel

I dispute that that is authoritarian, Frau Moltmann. There is no reason why you couldn't also put it in another way. But the charge that it is authoritarian is wrong.

Janowski

We can't resolve this issue now. I think that we should talk once again about the Spirit and fellowship. Philip Potter usually likes to describe the fellowship of Christians with an image from the First Letter of Peter, of the house of living stones. However, this house is now being increasingly built between two fronts: on the one hand fundamentalist groups, and on the other enthusiastic and charismatic movements. What Spirit will really blow through this house?

Potter

If the living stones are what they are in reference to Christ, then first of all ways and means must be found of living together. Different stones must be built into this living house.

Here I think that it's very important to have a sense of humour. If people take themselves too seriously and are no longer as open or as free as they would be if they belonged to Christ with all their convictions, then they cannot easily come together. But I believe that the real task is to bring together under one roof people who represent different views and who by listening to one another receive something from one another, and then also see that they do belong in the same house. We've really always had these very strict attitudes, and if that is the case then people retreat into their own corners and remain there. That certainly isn't the house of living stones. Perhaps they have different colours and forms, but Christ has formed them and made them part of this building. And it's great that we've experienced that in our church in the Caribbean.

Janowski
How can we renew this Spirit in our church, Professor Moltmann, if among us religion is in fact increasingly becoming a private matter? It's not so to speak a public doctrine that that is so, but such a trend can in fact be observed.

Moltmann
We've had religion in various political forms. In the Christian world, for centuries religion was a matter of state. From the time of the emperor Constantine onwards, Christianity was an imperial religion. After the Reformation there was the principle *cuius regio – eius religio:* the authorities determine the religion of the state. Only since the Enlightenment and the French Revolution has the human right to freedom of religion been discovered and established. The state has no competence in questions of religion. The decision lies with the individual. Consequently religion has been declared to be a 'private matter'. Today religion, too, is on offer in the global marketing of everything. It's becoming a 'commodity'

in the department of pastoral care. The modern 'multi-religious' society is a religious market society. People take from the various religions what they can use. The religions on offer no longer make any demands. That is Christian faith without the demands of the Sermon on the Mount or political discipleship. Faith in the crucified God doesn't fit into these political forms of religion. The one who was crucified by state power cannot easily become the God of a state religion. Religion may become a private matter, but not Christian faith as discipleship of the crucified Christ. Religion may well be marketed today, but Christian faith is recalcitrant. Why? Because we love life, and its dignity is more than a market value. The theology of the future may very well become a 'theology of life', for today life is fatally threatened by violence. A new 'reverence for life' and the will to protect it is coming into being inside and outside Christianity. Those who really love life break with the norms of the market society, for what one really loves cannot either be bought or sold.

Janowski
I wanted to ask you what is really meant by the vision of God and what we can understand by it today. That really belongs here. Christ didn't preach a private concern and religion in a corner, but the kingdom of God. What does that have to do with the church?

Moltmann
The Catholic modernist Alfred Loisy remarked, 'Jesus preached the kingdom of God and what came was the church.' That sounds like a disappointment, but it need not be. The church which is orientated on the universal kingdom of God understands itself as the vanguard, as the beginning and parable of the coming kingdom. The kingdom of God and his righteousness are universal. Therefore according to

the 1934 Barmen Theological Declaration of the Confessing Church the church must 'remind the rulers and the ruled' (and, I would add, the marketers and the marketed) 'of the kingdom and righteousness of God'. That is the public, prophetic task of the church of the kingdom of God, and for this we need a political or public theology. The expression 'kingdom of God' is a symbol. We can also describe what it means as 'life': whole, healed, accepted, eternal life. In the great dangers in which not only human life but the whole fabric of life on this earth is caught up, it is the task of those who believe and those who love to extend the great divine Yes to life, which we find in Christ and in the holy Spirit of life, arouse pleasure in living, and preserve the memory not only of suffering but also of resurrections.

Janowski
Unresolved problems, open questions. Some of these are really old questions which we've brought up now in the stocktaking by this generation, and which are posing themselves in a new and pointed form. Because many people find the churches joyless and void of content, and theology incomprehensible, they are setting off by themselves in search of inner support, seeking the meaning of their existence, and comfort in the face of the danger to their lives. For what a clearly tormenting awareness there is of our complicity in the impoverishment of many people near and far, and indifference to the exploitation of nature! We find it hard to see a way out of these dangers. We are told to keep going, but that isn't a way out; it's a catastrophe. Do Christian theologians and the church, we have to ask, really have some share in this development? Do they, too, bear some responsibility for the consequences, and will they accept this responsibility? And this despite the many moving testimonies and witnesses that there are in the church and academic theology? The theologians present here have accepted responsibility

and will continue to do so. They see before them a necessary transformation of the church, an exodus from the old walls, the old forms of life and the customary finances. A way will have to be found between the fronts of a secular world which has become religious and the civil religions of our national, post-industrial societies.

An Account of the Symposium

Hartmut Meesmann

The expression on Eberhard Jüngel's face says it all. Can it really be happening? The already downturned mouth turns down even further; there is a touch of frustration in the eyes; the hint of a furrowing of the brow; the face, kept completely straight, expresses defensiveness. This mimicry reflects the slightly pained question, 'Am I now actually to take up the gauntlet and begin the combat?'

Of course he wants to. Jüngel flirts a bit. The famous Protestant dogmatic theologian from Tübingen is merely pretending to hesitate, to be reluctant. At heart he loves a fight. And any rate he has the laughter on his side. And so he turns to his 'friend/foe' Dorothee Sölle, continues to tap the table energetically with the index finger of his right hand, and remarks, 'Politicizing of the conscience? Yes, but,' and the man rises to his full seated height, 'I am passionately opposed to another conscience telling me how my conscience is to judge.' The next sentence is almost a thunderclap. 'Conscience is always mine. That is what is conscientious about the conscience.' The Protestant has spoken.

Dorothee Sölle, sitting at the other end of the table, shakes her head vigorously. The feminist theologian from Hamburg, also a Protestant, leans over slightly towards her opponent, laughing, but with a sharp tone to her voice: 'What do you mean, conscience is always mine? I'm always bound up with a community.' And looking round at the audience of around four hundred, she asks: 'How far may individualism go?'

Conscience, sin – for Dorothee Sölle these concepts, rich in tradition, always primarily have a political dimension.

Jürgen Moltmann, sitting between the two, adopts the role of the mediator by offering an explanation. The man from Hamburg gently says that one cannot ignore the fact that each individual conscience is located in a collective 'blinkered context'. This leads to a tension: between the individual who judges on the one hand and the objective contradictions of society on the other.

But how does one deal with this tension in practice? The problem is not resolved this morning, nor is it discussed further.

Yet Eberhard Jüngel continues to look for a fight. He is clearly enjoying himself. Dorothee Sölle questions the omnipotence of God. A highly dubious position, Jüngel indicates by his tone of voice. He doesn't think that this omnipotence of God is completely 'obsolete' and refers to Martin Luther, who spoke of the empowering of human beings by God, the powerful God.

'Theology after Auschwitz?' He doesn't use this phrase, which is so central to Dorothee Sölle's work. 'I don't want to instrumentalize Auschwitz,' Jüngel explains briefly. But because the evil in the world is in fact an eminent challenge for the future and for human survival, he concerns himself with producing a 'table of categories of evil': one must look the enemy straight in the eye in order to be able to place him. In other words, one must know evil in order to stop it.

When Jürgen Moltmann remarks that the church and theology must finally bid farewell to the notion that religion is a private matter, Eberhard Jüngel angrily interjects, 'What theologian worth the name asserts that?' In his eyes this admonition from his former colleague on the faculty is a theological non-starter.

Yes, there were also arguments in this symposium in Tübingen which the Protestant theological faculty of the university arranged on the occasion of Jürgen Moltmann's seventieth birthday. It was a theological exhibition bout, partly staged for the public, but with a hard core of differences of opinion. Moreover it was a remarkable event: it had proved possible to assemble nine prominent theologians, men and women, leading figures of post-war theology, representatives of a generation of theologians which is now between sixty and seventy years old, at the same time and in the same place, under the calm and restrained chairmanship of the journalist Hans Norbert Janowski. They were there to discuss the question 'How I Have Changed'. Elisabeth Moltmann-Wendel, the wife of the man in whose honour the celebrations were, had had the idea. And there was a somewhat more academic subtitle: 'Biographical courses of theology in the second half of the twentieth century'.

The bright and friendly auditorium in the theological faculty building in Liebermeisterstrasse was packed to the doors; many people had to stand. The discussion was also broadcast to the lobby. But there was no really enormous crowd. Many young people had come and listened attentively. Would the professors in particular be capable of becoming really personal, and giving a vivid account of part of their individual theological development? They spoke in threes, in three rounds, on this eighth of June, which was a Saturday. And it was indeed an exciting day. Behind academic theology, sometimes more clearly and sometimes more indirectly, the person, the man or woman, with his or her life story, took on clearer contours. Though one always must bear in mind that such reconstructions of one's own life are always somewhat contrived, are constructions.

'Now you will see me go pale,' remarked Eberhard Jüngel, who spoke first. He was referring to Bertolt Brecht's story of Herr Keuner, which Jürgen Moltmann had mentioned in his introduction. In this short story Herr Keuner meets an acquaintance whom he has not seen for a long time. And when the acquaintance tells him that he, Keuner, hasn't changed at all, Herr Keuner goes pale.

'I too haven't changed', says Eberhard Jüngel with an impish look on his face. If one understands him rightly, he describes as his theological characteristic an unconditional obligation to the truth (of the gospel, but not just of the gospel). That is connected with his origins. Jüngel grew up in the former German Democratic Republic, in a home which showed no interest in religion. 'I discovered the Protestant church as the only place in the Stalinist society of East Germany,' he remarked, 'where one could speak the truth without being penalized, as in the cabaret.' Anyone who attempted to break with the compulsion to lie got involved with the secret police, as he did; at the beginning of the 1950s he fled from school because of critical remarks he made about society. 'Socialism was mendacious because one wasn't allowed to contradict. The church was the institutional place of truth.' No wonder that today Eberhard Jüngel says that for him the political dimension of Christianity lies 'in helping the truth to have its due rights'. That meanwhile Socialism as it existed in an East German form has collapsed is also a proof for the combative Tübingen systematic theologian that in the end the lie (as a system) does not establish itself.

But then the eloquent Protestant reveals to his attentive audience that personal experience of white racism in the South African townships has brought 'political theology' closer to him. Jüngel concedes that initially he had stormed against the 'clericalization of theology by the left wing', by political theology, but in South Africa he had 'learned better'. If need be, exclaims the man with the short grey-blond hair and the powerful voice, 'an inhuman situation must be changed by force', but that could only be decided subjectively by each individual.

Eberhard Jüngel had heard lectures by the philosopher

Martin Heidegger, and disputed with 'my teacher' Karl Barth, the controversial great Protestant church teacher, over a glass (or more) of wine. In contrast to Heidegger, Jüngel the theologian is firmly convinced that language must not fall silent in reflecting on God. 'Theology,' he says, 'must offer enlightenment in the light of the gospel, not of reason, but in critical dialogue with reason.' And it must concern itself more intensively with the phenomenon of evil if the earth is not to become hell.

Dorothee Sölle, who appears in a long turquoise summer dress, walking with a slight stoop, also finds in Tübingen those sharp formulations for which she is so well known: 'God's spirit doesn't blow in the theological faculties but in the protests against the transportation of nuclear waste', she says in her slightly fragile voice. And she had had 'the typical woman's career, i.e. none'. She speaks of her 'hostility to the church' in the early years (today she again has rather more hope for the church), of her aversion to theological 'muttering about the other world', her 'dismay' that after the Holocaust many theologians are simply going on as before. She tells of her teachers: Bultmann's pupil Marie Veit, who with great patience opened up theology to her; Friedrich Gogarten, who taught her 'to discard worn-out theological concepts'; and the exegete Ernst Käsemann, with whom it was 'not difficult' to dispute.

The grey-haired woman with the narrowed eyes tells of the 'Political Night Prayers' from the 1960s, that new form of worship in which information was given about events in politics and society and a call was issued for resistance and change. For Dorothee Sölle, this form of worship was a 'theological consequence of Auschwitz'. At that time we gained a new understanding of theological talk about sin,' she exclaims. 'What we fail to do separates us from God; that is sin.' In the Political Night Prayers the conscience was 'politicized'; it was here that 'political theology' came into being and was practised. It was a 'good time', Dorothee Sölle adds in a softer voice.

But this small, energetic woman was also shaped by feminism, which she got to know in the USA, and by ecumenism. She now regards theological talk of the 'omnipotence of God' as an expression of 'male delusions', as a masculine projection on to God. It took her thirty years to recognize this, she remarks. Feminist perspectives opened up to her a 'differentiated understanding of power': 'a good power is any power which empowers others', she explains. She is concerned with human dignity and greatness, which is in danger of being too quickly belittled before God.

She says that now she has given up the term 'political theology'; the 'theology of liberation' has taken its place. And by way of explaining what so impresses her about this theological trend, she cries out into the auditorium, 'We need people who interrupt! We must ask critical questions!'

At the end of her statement Dorothee Sölle confesses that nowadays a mystical understanding of the Christian faith has become important for her. She calls it the 'knowledge of God by way of experiment', a mysticism which is lived out in the everyday world of political resistance, in other words a relationship to God.

And then again there is a crystal-clear statement of the kind which makes Dorothee Sölle controversial for so many people, something which does not seem to disturb her any more, and which impresses yet others. In the face of the 'final victory of capitalism', she remarks, all that is left is Christian hope. Here is an expression of her mystical attitude in 1996.

Like Eberhard Jüngel and Dorothee Sölle, Jürgen Moltmann, too, the Protestant systematic theologian who has now retired, did not receive any religious upbringing in his parental home in Hamburg. The question of God emerged for him as a burning existential question – in a way not untypical for this generation, as we shall see – in the Second

World War. It took the form of a critical accusation and question, 'Where are you, God, in all this destruction and this misery?' Jürgen Moltmann tells us that he began to study theology in a prisoner of war camp, as the result of a personal encounter which shaped him and 'gave him courage', though he had really wanted to study mathematics and physics. 'So after the war I started to study theology in Göttingen, by candlelight because of the power cuts,' he says in a soft voice and in sentences which tumble out one after another. The church interested him less. Only the Confessing Church convinced him. Moltmann found his spiritual home there and in the community of the Brethren churches.

Shaped by Otto Weber, Dietrich Bonhoeffer, Christoph Blumhardt and Ernst Bloch among others – 'there is more in Protestantism than Karl Barth' – Moltmann developed a particular theological sense for the social and political dimension of Christian faith. His key phrases are 'kingdom of God theology' and 'worldly preaching of God'. 'That gave me much support in my life,' remarks the short, rather distinguished looking man with the dark-rimmed spectacles.

Jürgen Moltmann's book *Theology of Hope* made him widely known. 'I didn't want to baptize Ernst Bloch's *Principle of Hope*, but I wanted to open up a parallel discussion within theology.' The theologian gives these reasons for writing the book and then goes on to utter the following *bon mot*: 'After the change in East Germany I found one of the most perceptive reviews of my book in the archives of the secret police. The reviewer judged that the book was too revolutionary for East German Christians.' Laughter from the audience.

Jürgen Moltmann, who with his wife initiated this symposium, then enumerates in rapid succession important stages which have prompted him to theological insights and reactions: for example the Christian-Marxist dialogue within the Paulusgesellschaft; the thrusting slogan 'Dare more democracy' in the period of the social liberal upheaval associated with the SPD politician and former chancellor Willy Brandt; the brutal end to the 'Prague Spring' in 1968; the incomprehensible encyclical on the pill, *Humanae vitae*; the Second Vatican Council with new perspectives for ecumenism; the murder of the black leader Martin Luther King. And Moltmann then concedes: 'My great hope that a socialism with a human face and social democracy could come together has been disappointed.'

For this creative Protestant thinker, too – 'I was always somewhat one-sided' – the recognition that theology after Auschwitz must be different from theology before the annihilation of the Jews has become fundamental. In this context his question was: is God incapable of suffering? It led to his book *The Crucified God*, which develops the message of the God who suffers with us. 'For my question was: what does the cross of Christ mean for God himself?'

It is striking that Jürgen Moltmann – like Dorothee Sölle, Johann Baptist Metz or Norbert Greinacher – found important stimuli for his 'theological existence' in Latin America. Moltmann acknowledges that a 'turning point' in his life came when he took part in a conference of theologians in 1977. 'There I recognized,' he says, 'that I didn't belong anywhere, since I'm not oppressed, not black and not a woman.' So in Germany he turned to the peace movement and the environmental movement and became committed in them and for them, in order to give expression to what he calls a 'theology of life'.

At the end of his rapidly presented thoughts Jürgen Moltmann gives a simple answer to the question which he put to himself about his fundamental motive for theological work: 'curiosity'.

Johann Baptist Metz, the Catholic theologian now teaching in Vienna – along with Jürgen Moltmann he is one of the founders of political theology – had mocked the curiosity of this Protestant theologian the night before the symposium, when they were all sitting together drinking a glass of wine and arguing: 'You know more about the inner life of God than you do about that of your Elisabeth,' remarked Metz to peals of laughter from those listening to the nocturnal dispute. Moltmann replied, 'And I just can't understand, dear Baptist, why you want to know so little about God.'

The bell goes for the second round, and after the brief pause the hall is full again. It is now above all Johann Baptist Metz who makes it clear how much a fundamental experience in the war has shaped his theological thought. 'Pressed' into the army at the age of sixteen, one day he had been sent off by his company commander to take a message. When he got back he found all his comrades dead, the victims of an allied attack. 'I remember my silent cry,' remarks Metz in the tense silence of the auditorium. 'This silent cry has persisted to the present day,' adds the man with the round face and the deep voice, which is why he has come to speak at this symposium about what has not changed for him in his life. At that time all his childhood dreams, which had formed on the soil of his powerful Bavarian homeland, collapsed. 'The category of danger has become central for me,' he says, and at the same time he explains why for him 'sensitivity to theodicy', a sense of the almost unanswerable question why God allows suffering in the world, has become the most important mark of identity for a convincing theology. 'That,' says Metz, taking up Jüngel's statement, is 'my perspective on the truth' in theology.

And the phrase 'theology after Auschwitz' appears in Metz's remarks, too. It is bound up with the question of the suffering of others, including the suffering of the unatoned-for victims of history. That above all concerns him. 'Does theology heal all wounds?' asks the theologian. He puts this question in such a way that the answer can only be 'No'.

For Metz, too, the great challenge lies in incorporating the experiences, insights and complaints of the men and women (and the theologians) of the so-called Third World into his theological work. Metz, who becomes particularly lively and spontaneous when he is speaking extempore, concedes that he 'bit off more than he could chew' when he saw the model of the base church as this developed in Latin America as being also a model for the future of the church in Europe.

Today, he tells his audience in Tübingen, the important thing is to perceive the pain and suffering all over the world with sensitivity, but without falling into a romanticism of suffering. 'Do we have a culture,' asks the former Münster professor, 'which acknowledges the mysteries of others, of other cultures?'

Johann Baptist Metz, who loves a good phrase and as a result sometimes develops a very distinctive language, mentions as a scarlet thread in his biography the *memoria passionis*, the recollection of suffering. 'The Christian message of redemption does not settle this question,' he impresses on his hearers, 'it remains the silent cry before the dark countenance of God.' As the question 'Why?' goes unanswered, all that is left is prayer, as a lament, as a cry.

A new, quite different, accent comes into the discussion with Elisabeth Moltmann-Wendel. It is not surprising that later she carries on a small argument with Metz or he with her. For at present this feminist theologian will have nothing to do with guilt, original sin and suffering. Quite the contrary. The 'theology of corporeality' which has recently become so important for her is about totality, about beauty, about being accepted, about the social dignity of the body, which today is threatened by torture, poverty and sexual violence. It is also about self-love, acceptance of one's own person and one's own body. Metz will later take up this term.

Now Elisabeth Moltmann-Wendel is sitting between Metz and Norbert Greinacher in a white summer costume. With rosy cheeks she tells how her family was shaped by the

Confessing Church, among other things united in a resolute rejection of the National Socialists; how she carried around with her a picture of Pastor Niemöller as 'a mixture of icon and mascot'; how she had been rather mistrustful of the church, but then began her studies in Berlin in 1945 with Protestant theology. Later she went to Göttingen, 'the Mecca of a theology which is critical of politics and the church'. 'At that time,' she says with a smile, 'Tübingen seemed too pious and unpolitical to me.'

In 1951, unmarried, she gained her doctorate with Otto Weber in Göttingen and became *virgo doctissima*, a learned virgin, as the faculty's doctoral certificate put it. However, her marriage to Jürgen Moltmann soon afterwards barred her way to the career of a pastor, to which she aspired. At that time there were celibacy clauses in the Protestant church, too.

This morning, while a thunderstorm slowly broods outside, Elisabeth Moltmann-Wendel shows most clearly how much she has changed in her biography. Marriage, children, housework – that 'paralysed' her theological interest. 'My personality was stifled', is how she describes her situation at that time, with some humour. 'My existence and theology no longer had any points of contact.' A woman's fate.

Only when the children were older was she again stimulated from outside: she mentions the human rights discussion in the USA, the new understanding of partnership between husband and wife which was dawning – one can only guess at what new perspectives must have opened up at that time in this marriage of theologians. 'So around 1968,' she related, 'theologians were suddenly discussing grass-roots democracy, monopolistic state capitalism, the imperative mandate. The women's movement became a topic. My world did a complete U-turn. I was no longer a wife and mother.'

And then, as Elisabeth Moltmann-Wendel puts it, she 'wrote herself free', working on all her personal themes in books. Here her slogan was to become her own person, to detach herself from the influence of others, to discover a new self-awareness as a woman, to live out her own identity. She acquired her own profession, as a feminist theologian attempting to mediate between the fronts. 'It was and is important to help self-love to have its due in the church as well,' she proclaims to the auditorium, that self-love which the Reformer Calvin once called a 'harmful pestilence'.

'Self-love,' says Johann Baptist Metz hesitantly and reflectively in the round of discussion which follows, 'is rather difficult. I am not happy with my perception of myself.' To this man, what the theological friend sitting next to him has said is somewhat suspect, at least problematical. 'God doesn't make me happy; that's the result of my perception of myself,' he then says quite openly. 'Was Jesus happy with his Father?' One may certainly ask that, says the Catholic priest and professor of theology, turning to his audience, who listen all day quietly and attentively. He's not certain here. 'Everything need not always be good,' he comments, expressing his critical scepticism about Elisabeth Moltmann-Wendel's call for the positive.

She twice asks her Catholic colleague, pressing him in a friendly way, what place corporeality has in his theology. Metz, loud and rebellious, half in jest and half in earnest, points out that he wrote about this at a very early stage. 'And you've quoted it,' he adds in an undertone, as if to say, 'Give it a rest.'

Then Metz defends himself against possibly appearing as a theologian who torments himself. 'No, no,' he says, 'suffering isn't fantastic, isn't a sign of love. Suffering is painful, and it leads to nothingness.' And he criticizes Dorothee Sölle and Jürgen Moltmann for having made themselves a 'concept of suffering' too early. He warns against superelevating suffering in an aesthetic way.

Metz makes clear once again the political relevance of his

appeal to perceive the suffering of others sensitively by taking the war in Yugoslavia as an example. The people were destroying one another because they merely looked back on their own past of suffering and were incapable of also seeing the history of the suffering of others (other ethnic groups).

Metz then takes up what is at present probably the most controversial topic among theologians, the question whether God is really omnipotent. Talk of the God who shows solidarity cannot resolve the problem of God's omnipotence either, Metz objects to Jürgen Moltmann. The God who shows solidarity is also ultimately a victor, and the God who shows solidarity also has power. Thus the notion of the omnipotence of God cannot be settled so simply in theological terms. The man who teaches theology in the Romano Guardini chair in Vienna wants to maintain the notion of the omnipotent God, as does Eberhard Jüngel.

'I am grateful to Jürgen Moltmann and Johann Baptist Metz,' says Norbert Greinacher, the third speaker in this second round of discussion, 'and I say that here quite openly.' With their politically orientated theology these two colleagues had 'opened a door' for him. That was in the 1960s. 'My father was a university professor, but politics was completely alien.' Greinacher, who still has another year to teach Catholic pastoral theology in Tübingen before he retires, remarks that his family was 'ultra-conservative, the most conservative imaginable'. This man, now white-haired, grew up in Catholic Freiburg, studied theology there and became a priest.

Greinacher identifies the stages of his life by theological concepts. At the beginning came 'universal theology', 'incredible experiences'; in Paris; getting to know the worker priests; theological inspiration from Cardinal Daniélou, who was then in Paris; and later encounters in Vienna with Eastern European theologians and theologies. 'I noticed,'

Greinacher sums up in his precise voice, 'that there was something other than neoscholastic German theology.'

There followed his discovery of political theology and later that of liberation theology. A very important experience was his encounter with the liberation theologians Gustavo Gutierrez and Leonardo Boff, whom he came to know through his collaboration in the international theological journal *Concilium*. 'That was when my love for Latin America was born,' remarks this apparently somewhat melancholy theologian, who in the subsequent period led a number of study trips to the American continent.

The Protestant milieu of the Swabian city of Tübingen to which he came as professor in 1969 'has suited me well', says Greinacher. It brought him closer to the ecumenical dimension of theology. In recent years it has dawned on him how important the 'prophetic element' was for early Christianity, and this leads him to raise the question of the prophetic in the church.

Then Greinacher becomes reflective. He speaks haltingly. For he acknowledges: 'I used to have an unquestioning faith and a fundamentally unquestioning theology. But in recent years I have lost such a faith and theology.' Why? This man who is often reviled in his church is clearly now particularly concerned with the question 'Why suffering?' He mentions the great earthquake of Lisbon in the eighteenth century; mentions the genocide of millions of Indios in the sixteenth century; mentions the Jewish Holocaust in the twentieth century. The New Testament seems to give him a little support in his doubt. 'If even Jesus' disciples doubted, as the Bible reports,' says Norbert Greinacher, 'then perhaps a theologian, too, may be allowed to have some doubts.'

Unfortunately Philip Potter, the black theologian from Jamaica, is hardly personal. This man, who for a long time was General Secretary of the World Council of Churches (WCC), opens the last round of discussion after the lunch break and a great rainstorm. He fuses his own biography above all with the political and theological development of the World Council in Geneva. He has a good knowledge of German theology. Wearing a grey-blue summer suit, he traces above all, in English, the history of the World Council of Churches: the discovery of the world-wide base movements, contextual theology, the liberation movements throughout the world, the peace movement, the international ecumenical movement. He recalls the world-wide struggle for human rights, the programme for a new society of men and women in the church, and pleads afresh for a critical attitude of the churches to the exploitative structures in the economy against the background of the misery in the poor and under-developed countries of the so-called Third World. Philip Potter has often been involved in shaping this development and has introduced his theological emphases into the sometimes difficult discussions in the World Council of Churches. He describes the prophetic objections of the church in the economic sphere as the 'most critical and important' challenge, since many governments are 'slaves of the economy rather than servants of humankind'. The poor, he emphatically declaims, must not keep getting poorer and the rich richer.

What the man from the Caribbean, who now lives with his German wife in Stuttgart, makes clear is that at that time, in the 1960s, he and many others developed the Christian faith afresh by holding 'the Bible in one hand and the newspaper in the other'. In other words, for Philip Potter, too, the discovery of the social and political dimension and relevance of faith was an important experience and a guideline for his own action.

But Eberhard Jüngel and Hans Küng do not have such good words for the World Council of Churches. Jüngel had said in his statement that it was a 'scandal' that the World Council of Churches had developed no liberation theology for Eastern Europe which took Russian Orthodoxy into account. Philip Potter can only reply by referring to the well-known practice of 'silent diplomacy' in which the World Council of Churches engaged.

Hans Küng, too, fires some big guns. He speaks of the 'unholy alliance between the Vatican and the WCC' when it comes to excluding critical spirits for diplomatic reasons. 'I have never been invited to the World Council of Churches,' mocks the Swiss theologian, who in his outspoken way opposes any pussyfooting in the church.

Nor is pussyfooting the style of Jörg Zink, the Protestant journalist and television pastor, who right at the start describes himself as a 'grubby street urchin', his way of describing the fact that he is not a college teacher. This man, too, with his tanned face, snow-white hair and piercing eyes, who can put things so grippingly, describes the emergence of political theology as 'a liberation for me'. 'The need for political collaboration' has strengthened him throughout his life, he remarks. Zink helped to build up the Green Party, and became involved in the peace movement and the ecology movement; over the years this heightened the tensions with the church authorities. The inexorable consequence was that in 1980 Zink left the service of the church.

'Feminist liberation theology has become important to me,' the theologian continues, and then goes on to mention his mother, who in his youth spoke to him of the 'right woman in every man, who must not be neglected'. Immediately after the war, in that 'atmosphere of confused restoration', psychological and therapeutic approaches in theology tended to be mocked. Jörg Zink includes that in the 'bad preparation for the times to come' which he now complains about in retrospect.

The conviction has grown in him, he continues, that the confessions are obsolete. 'The confessions are deader than they believe, and today we are going out beyond the remains of their walls.' He has also left behind Karl Barth's *Church Dogmatics*. He quotes Eberhard Jüngel, who once said, 'The truth cannot be as long as that – 8,000 pages.' He would also like to leave behind him, he remarks, the current 'reactionary' relationship between state and church in Germany. Jörg Zink truly does not mince his words.

Like Dorothee Sölle, this 'impatient loner' (his own words) has also rediscovered mysticism. This is a mysticism which knows itself to be lovingly and respectfully bound up with God's creation, for which a plant is more important than any book. Zink says that with this rediscovery of mysticism he has found a way back to his 'old roots'. The rediscovery of the mystical language of images is important to this man who calls the Catholic theologian and philosopher Romano Guardini his 'most important teacher'. Anyone who is concerned with images can expand the verbose theistic Christian spirituality which is completely orientated on God. Then comes a typical comment: 'The right-hand side of a theologian's brain must be more than a dried plum!'

Has he changed? Zink remarks that he has not run after particular theological fashions, nor does he recommend that. His plea, which is authenticated by his life, is rather, 'One must keep always being recognized as the same person.'

Hans Küng picks up this thread. '*Semper idem*, always the same,' remarks the former Director of the Tübingen Institute for Ecumenical Research, is not his motto. However, this saying was engraved on the coat of arms of his first great opponent, the Italian Curia Cardinal Ottaviani, once head of the Holy Roman Inquisition, now the Congregation of Faith. Certainly identity is called for, but not conformity, he remarks in his typical way. Verging on seventy, with waved grey hair and a rumpled, almost furrowed brow, he begins immediately to make his church-political and theological points in a combative way.

It was truly impossible to fool him, he exclaimed restlessly and full of energy; he was the 'archetypal insider', and knew this Roman Catholic system back to front. None of his colleagues 'even here in Tübingen' dared to grasp the problem of papal infallibility. They knew what they would be in for, he adds smugly. Küng refers to his book *Infallible? An Enquiry*, and says, 'That is the book that I would like to write again today.' He doesn't withdraw an iota of his critical enquiry.

A pupil above all of Karl Rahner, Henri de Lubac and Yves Congar, the Protestant tenet of 'justification of the sinner before God by faith alone' has become central for him. 'That,' remarks the former conciliar theologian Küng, 'is my existence: one is not justified before God by works, not even by theological works.'

The next attack: he is disappointed that this morning there was no mention of the historical criticism of the Bible to which progressive theology owes its essential insights – and that is also true of him personally. The gulf between exegesis and dogmatics is still manifest. 'Do you believe,' he asks his colleagues, 'that you can provide a biblical basis for the Trinity?' 'Yes,' shouts out Eberhard Jüngel, now sitting in the audience in the second row. The audience laughs. Hans Küng retorts, 'That's how we get apologetic answers without any basis.' More general laughter. If they had time, the two theologian friends would certainly have wanted to continue this skirmish. One can only guess at how they argue in domestic surroundings.

Hans Küng goes on to say that the need for church reform should not be as underestimated as it is in liberation theology. They could yet have some surprises. The World Council of Churches again gets what is coming to it; many Christians would still assent to the statement that no salvation is to be found outside the church – 'and the World Council of Churches doesn't dare to tackle this theme', he remarks, with a glance at Philip Potter. But Potter has not been General Secretary for a long time.

At the end of his statement Hans Küng sums up his theological concern like this. He has always been concerned 'to integrate' the various theological trends and approaches; that has been his specifically 'Catholic' way. Then he cannot resist another teasing thrust: 'I slowly get on with my theological work and don't jump from topic to topic, like Jürgen Moltmann.' Moltmann hears this and smiles.

The last remark of this Tübingen dogmatic theologian and priest, whose church withdrew his licence to teach in 1979 and who has still made no formal moves to reverse what he regards as an unjustified measure, is: 'I enjoy theological work, and I hope to continue to do so for a long time.'

But some time, in the not very distant future, these theologians, men and women, will – unfortunately – have retired. Then, as we are already realizing in Tübingen, an era will be at an end. Then these teachers – idiosyncratic and striking personalities, each in his or her own way – will have shaped the generations of Christians and also have left important and always highly controversial marks on their churches. They will be memorable, indispensable figures in the history of theology . . . one hopes not too soon.

Models, leaders, are also being called for today. But they have become scarcer. Also among theologians, at least those who can challenge a broad public in society and the church. That in itself is a pity.